ERNA AND THE TOKYO WAR TRIALS

by Stephen P. Cano

Printed in the United States of America
first printing

ISBN 979-8-999723-30-7

Design and production services for this book were provided by Linden Publishing, Fresno, CA. 800-345-4447.

Contents

For Erna

Beatrice, Nebraska.

1

Beatrice, Nebraska

In 1914 postage stamps cost $0.02, a pound loaf of bread cost $0.06, a quart of milk cost $0.09 and a house cost $4,615. Henry Ford announced he'd give workers $5 a day. The Boston Braves took the World Series over Philadelphia in four games and Woodrow Wilson was President. And in Beatrice, Nebraska, Erna Elizabeth Warkentin was born to Cornelius Warkentin and Margaret Bergeman.

Much of Erna's early life influences were found in her Mennonite upbringing and in her school experiences. She was a product of Beatrice Public Schools. Erna attended Beatrice Junior High school which was a gorgeous two-story building including twenty-one classrooms, library, auditorium (seating 1,256), gymnasium and offering a demanding curriculum. Erna eventually moved on to Beatrice Senior High School, another beautiful building with sixteen regular classrooms. Erna was a member of the Beatrice Chapter National Honor Society. She also attended the University of Nebraska and George Washington.

Friends played a huge part in Erna's early childhood. One friend, Evelyn Korbeliki, recalled living on a farm in Beatrice. Often, during the summer, Erna and a friend, Lois, would walk out to Evelyn's house. Erna would call beforehand and then Evelyn would hustle and make food for lunch and some ice cream afterwards. They would sit out on the lawn under huge pine trees. Sometimes they sewed. One summer they made gorgeous lounging pajamas out of the most gavish and loudest and cheapest fabrics they could find. Evelyn's were morning glories and the flowers were huge. Erna had pansies or carnations, also huge.

They were as close as family. All during their school years, Erna's mother would invite Evelyn for lunch on her birthday. Evelyn could choose the dessert and often Erna's mother made the most delicious desserts such as floating island or custard with caramel sauce.

A look at Erna's Class of 1931 Baccalaureate Service drama play also gives insight into her generation influences. Their play was titled, "The Importance of Being Earnest." The Baccalaureate Service also had a sermon and on the back of the program Erna wrote her notes from the sermon and mentioned the four things a man must do if he would make his record true. The first is to think without confusion, clearly. The second is to love his fellow man, sincerely. The third was to act from honest motives, purely. And the fourth was to trust God in Heaven, securely. Often times, Erna's generation is called the greatest generation but it is usually said in context of our men soldiers. Those men had mothers and wives and sisters and they all played a role in America's struggle to overcome the great depression and win victory in WWII.

Erna in Washington D.C., 1943.

Shortly after graduating from Beatrice High School, Erna was hired as a Dental Assistant and worked in this capacity until 1939. Her boss described Erna's character as including qualities of fidelity and confidence which were exemplary.

He also said she was a good Christian young lady whose character cannot be challenged. The character traits would be called upon by her government in later years in ways Erna could not fathom in 1939.

The year 1939 would usher in changes in Erna's life that would take her on the greatest adventures of her life. Like a calling from afar, Erna would lift her eyes for a better life and be swept into some of the most historical events in American history.

In 1940, Erna's friend, Evelyn Korbelok, was living in Omaha, Nebraska with her new husband, who was in medical school. The phone rang and Erna told Evelyn she was in Omaha waiting for a train. She had time to wait at the station so she came out to Evelyn's apartment. Erna said she had quit her job and was going to Washington, D.C. She didn't have a job but had made up her mind to go and seek a better and more rewarding life. They talked for a long time. Evelyn felt if she had been in Erna's shoes, she would have been so nervous. She reached over and felt Erna's pulse. It was as calm as if it were an ordinary moment. Both Evelyn and her husband, Ed, went with Erna to the train station. Evelyn would never forget that day. She was deeply moved by Erna's courage and confidence in her own ability. Evelyn had so much respect for Erna, so did her husband, Ed.

Erna in Washington, DC, 1943.

Erna arrived in Washington D.C. in early 1940 and promptly landed a job with the U.S. Dept, of Agriculture as secretary to the Section Chief and then secretary to the Division Chief. From June 1942 to July 1945, Erna worked at the Foreign Economic Administration and focused on importing for the war effort. She also found time to graduate from the American National Red Cross in May 1944.

3

Erna's Red Cross graduating class, May 1944.

Erna's Red Cross diploma, May 1944.

2

Erna's Top Secret Mission—Joint Intelligence Objectives Agency

In July 1945, Erna received an assignment that would place her in the middle of one of the most top secret programs in American history. Erna joined the Joint Intelligence Objectives Agency (JIOA). The top secret program was called Operation Paperclip. It was a postwar U.S. intelligence program that eventually brought German scientist to America under secret military contracts. Operation Paperclip began in May 1945 and Erna started in July 1945. This agency was sponsored by the Joint Chiefs of Staff, State Department, War, Navy, Foreign Economic Associations, etc. for purposes of learning what progress in industry and science had been

Paris, Early 1946. Erna and the JIOA Group. Erna is second from right.

made by Germany during war years when avenues for such information were closed to the U.S. stenographers.

After helping with two such reports in London, Erna was transferred to the Hochst office in Germany where her assignment was secretary to one of the men who acted as coordinator of a group of investigations. The Joint Intelligence Objectives Agency (JIOA) was created solely and specifically to recruit and hire Nazi scientist and put them on weapons projects and in scientific intelligence programs within the Army, the Navy, the Air Force, the CIA (starting in 1947), and other organizations.

Erna stayed in the London JIOA office until October 11, 1945. On October 12th she left London on a Special flight military aircraft to Hochst, Germany for permanent duty in the Hochst JIOA office. She was given a baggage allowance of 100 lbs. Authority was granted to carry photographic equipment. Erna was also a designated Official Courier for the purpose of carrying classified documents.

Erna was able to read, speak and understand the German language and this undoubtedly came in handy during her time spent working in the JIOA. Although initially there was some resistance to the JIOA program within the military, as soon as the Soviet Union started grabbing Nazi scientist off the streets of Germany, everyone realized how critical it was to get to the German scientist before the Soviets could grab them.

Top secret JIOA compound entrance. Hochst,
Germany, 1945–1946.

R E S T R I C T E D

7:00 AM.
18 Old Quebec Street
Flight. Special # 4

HEADQUARTERS
UNITED KINGDOM BASE
APO 413, US ARMY

AF/hs

AG. 230.36 L10-661

11 October 1945.

SUBJECT: Orders

TO: MR HENRY O. BABB, Civilian,
        MR FRITZ O. KOEPLER, Civilian,
        MR HENRY L. MUOL, Civilian,
        MISS HELEN CARLE, Civilian,
        MISS ERNA L. JORGENTIN, Civilian,
        MR WALTER M. POLLITZER, Civilian,

1. Civilians named above, FIAT (Office of Mil. Gov. for Germany)
London, will proceed on or about 15 October 1945, by military aircraft,
surface T, and/or rail, from present station to Hochst, Germany, for
permanent duty.
2. A baggage allowance of one hundred (100) lbs is atzd the above
named Civilians.
3. Authority is granted to carry photographic equipment.
4. Civilians named above are designated Official Courier for the
purpose of carrying classified documents.
5. TCNT. ILN. PCS. 60-136 114 P 431-02-03 A 212/60425.

BY COMMAND OF BRIGADIER GENERAL STRONG:

Allen Freeman

ALLEN FREEMAN,
CWO, USA,
Assistant Adjutant General

DISTRIBUTION:

FIAT, London..................... 45
  Each Civilian...........(6)
AG Orders 1
AG Records 1

R E S T R I C T E D

Erna's restricted flight orders to Hochst,
Germany, October 1945.

Top secret JIOA compound entrance. Hochst,
Germany, 1945–1946.

Erna in Taunus Mountains, JIOA, Hochst, 1945.

On January 15, 1946, Erna completed her assignment in Hochst, Germany and returned to the United States via London. All movement was restricted and top secret. Erna received a letter from the London office of the Joint Intelligence Objectives Agency. In the letter, the Chief of the JIOA Group, George L. Powell, expressed his gratitude to Erna for the services she rendered to their organization. Chief Powel indicated Erna's task was accomplished under difficult conditions in a war torn Europe. He said Erna's understanding, co-operation and diligent efforts had been invaluable to the work of the Joint Intelligence Objectives Agency.

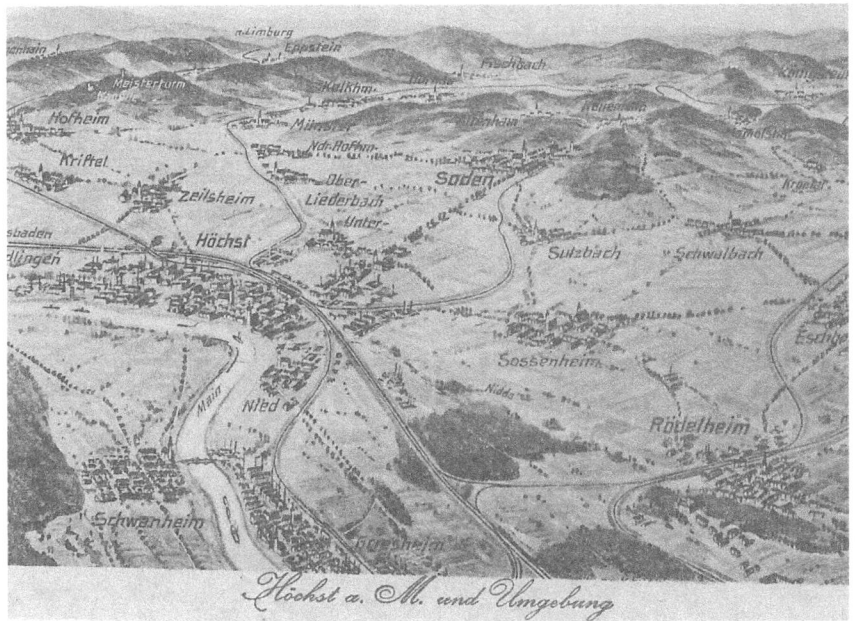

Map of Hochst, Germany.

On May 6, 1946, the War Department issued travel orders to Erna. She was directed to proceed by air on May 8, 1946, from Washington, D.C. to Hamilton Field, California for further movement by air, on about May 10, 1946, to Tokyo, Japan, on permanent duty.

Erna was hired by the War Department, International Prosecution Section. The International Prosecution Section was established as a

Portrait of Erna, Christmas 1945, Germany.

THE FOREIGN SERVICE
OF THE
UNITED STATES OF AMERICA

AMERICAN EMBASSY
ECONOMIC WARFARE DIVISION.
40, BERKELEY SQUARE · W.1.
TELEPHONE · GROSVENOR 4961.

January 15, 1946

Miss Erna Warkentin,
Technical Industrial Intelligence Branch,
Joint Intelligence Objectives Agency,
Room 2213,
Munitions Building,
Constitution Avenue,
Washington, D.C.

Dear Miss Warkentin,

On behalf of the London office of the Joint
Intelligence Objectives Agency I should like to express
my gratitude to you for the services you have rendered
our organization.

Yours has been a task accomplished under
difficult conditions in a war torn Europe. Your understanding,
co-operation and diligent efforts have been invaluable to
the work of the Joint Intelligence Objectives Agency.

Many thanks and the best of luck to you.

Sincerely yours,

George L. Powell
Chief JIOA Group

Letter from JIOA Group Chief George L. Powell to Erna.

special staff section to prepare for trial and prosecute all cases involving crime resulting from planning, preparing, initiating, or waging of a war of aggression or a war in violation of international treaties and agreements, or participation in a common plan or conspiracy for the accomplishment of any of the forgoing. The trial would last two and a half years.

Her boss would be the Acting Chief Prosecutor, Frank Tavenner. She was employed as a stenographer to aid in legal work pertaining to prosecution of war criminals. She began the assignment working for various attorneys on staff. During the last months of her contract she served as secretary to Mr. Tavenner who was then acting as Chief Prosecutor in place of the Prosecutor who was temporarily in the United States for an extended period of time due to illness. Her duties included coordinating activities of staff and gathering of necessary data for presentation of case, all under the direction of Mr. Tavenner. Erna would work for the IPS (International Prosecution Section) for about one year. Her time spent in Japan was documented by an extraordinary preservation of letters Erna sent from Japan to the U.S. This is Erna's story in her own words.

3

Erna Departs for Japan

May 27, 1946[1]   Dear Relatives and Friends—   For most of you, I can start reporting from the time I arrived at Hamilton Field, California. I arrived there about 9:30 in the evening and finally disposed of my parachute harness, which I had to wear all the way across the country. Hamilton Field is huge and it seemed we drove and drove to get to my quarters. It was nothing special, more or less barracks style. There were a few USO girls there, waiting to fly out, and two army nurses just in from the Pacific (one of whom was to call you, Jeri, and report my arrival). Thinking I had no time to lose on calling people in San Francisco, I tried to find a phone nearby, without luck. The Foreign Priorities office was closed so I had to stay on the Field until morning. However, I got up at daybreak with the aforementioned nurse and we had breakfast together. I might as well have slept for they had a schedule of appointments which kept me on the Field all day, a new smallpox shot, "ditching movie" (I'm making carbons, and the time is of the essence, so I'll not erase mistakes unless they are too bad). I signed papers and more papers and in between tried to coax the powers that be to not put me on the "alert" list for at least another day. But, no, when it was posted at 4 o'clock, there my name was so I had to weigh in. You really are not supposed to leave the field once alerted, but my coaxing at least had this much effect, I left the place at 5 o'clock and stayed in San Francisco until about four the next afternoon. In that time, I had dinner at the Clift downtown S.F. at night and ended up at the Top of the Mark.

The next morning we had a leisurely late breakfast, went shopping and I cheated a bit by adding the weight of a new evening dress to my luggage, from I. Magnin. Then we went thru Chinatown and up to Telegraph Hill. I checked in at the Terminal at 5:30 to find the flight had been delayed another three hours, so I made a couple more calls, wrote some letters

---

1 Erna Warkentin letter, May 27, 1946.

and had dinner, and donned my Mae West (parachute harness). We had to wear those all the way across, but only at take-off and landing times. I was the only girl on the plane to Hickham Field, and I couldn't have asked for better attention from the Flight Clerk. We dropped down at Hickham about 8:30 a.m. and had about four hours there. Having eaten on the plane, I wasn't hungry, so I checked out a towel and took a shower, then generally looked the place over and broke down to have my last real hamburger and milk shake.

Erna working the IPS Tokyo Trials.

The flight to Johnson Island was just four hours. The approach to that island is perfectly beautiful. The island is only a pinpoint of sand in the midst of a very blue ocean and the coral reefs throw a variety of colors just bordering the island. That is as far as I can go. Once down it loses all appeal and must be a deadly place to be stationed, scarcely any vegetation. We were taken up to the Officer's Mess to eat and our driver told us that the traffic regulations are so strict he was fined the other day for passing a stop sign. The fine was 10 dollars I believe he said. The amazing thing is that the way the streets and stop signs are laid out would allow any MP to patrol the island from any given spot. I guess you'd better be good there.

After about an hour we took off for Kwajalein. At Johnson I locked up my camera, for just out of Kwaj the Flight Clerk picks up any in sight and turns them in to the Captain of the plane. Supposedly the next crew's Captain returns them when you are well out of there, but I wasn't taking any chances. The reason for taking the cameras is that absolutely no pictures are allowed there due to the proximity of the atomic bomb tests. We landed there late at night and it was about there that we crossed the International Date Line. We practically lost Sunday. No criticism from anyone, please, for my not going to church.

I did see some of the boats which will take part in the atomic tests, but the darkness precluded seeing very much. Out of Kwaj a little ways it must have been rough for I suddenly awakened. The Flight Clerk had said that the Captain would let us up on the flight deck, so I thought that an excellent opportunity. The clerk asked the Captain who said he hadn't been home for five days, but I could come at my own risk. I spent over half an hour up there. I watched the navigator shoot the stars, saw the automatic pilot, watched the radio man and got quite a kick out of it. While I was up there we flew through a storm and the rain pounded all sides of the cockpit but it only lasted a few minutes. I picked a good time. Folks who went up in the daytime were only allowed to stay about five minutes. We landed at Guam about 8:30 in the morning and they said for me to go to the billeting area. So after having breakfast with some of the GI's, on the plane (incidentally most of the passengers were air corps GI's, scarcely any brass), I hopped a jeep and went on up to where the flight nurses are billeted. Any passing females also stayed here. I was a bit puzzled for I was scheduled to have only three hours there. It turned into three days. Four civilian girls had just arrived for permanent duty. Apparently they were the first in that section of the island. The personnel officer had given them two days to get adjusted. So we grabbed a jeep since you simply can't walk from one place to another there. They took me in and the first day the personnel officer took several of us to the beach, Tumon Bay. It is a very nice beach, lined with palm trees and nice sand. I got a good dose of the sun. I actually got too much sun but I didn't know then I'd have two more days and I was getting as much as I could.

That night we were supposed to meet this officer at the lounge of the officer's mess. I was supposed to eat at the transient mess at the terminal but all agreed that was not the thing to do so they arranged for me to be a "guest" of one of them. The officer brought along a couple of very nice friends. One of whom became my guide and protector from then on. He really was a lot of fun. We all drove down to the other end of the island that night and saw the navy base and some of the native stuff en route. The bar at the lounge closed at 9:30 but the nurses had some kind of delivery system and we could get beer and cokes from the icebox in our billet. We had a sort of lounge, primitive though it was. So we all usually ended up there until our curfew of 12 o'clock.

The second day we girls went to the beach alone. That night two couples of us went to the outdoor movies. The moon was so full that the screen wasn't too clear. All the ATC (Air Transport Command) quarters are up on a hill overlooking the airstrip and Tumon Bay. The lounge and mess have windows almost reaching the floor. So you can imagine the view is pretty much all right. At dinner the second night I was lamenting the fact that there would be no one for me to play with the next day. Therefore I hoped I would depart for Tokyo. My friend Ken said to not worry because he would get time off from the office and take me swimming. So we had a nice swim. That evening we went to a dance down at the other end of the island.

The next day he had arranged for one of his friends to take me swimming and in the evening there was going to be a big picnic. The P&T officer had said there wasn't a chance of my getting out. They kept kidding me about "fixing" the manifest. If so, someone slipped, for I had scarcely turned out the light the third night when the Nurse in charge of our quarters called to say the word had just come through that she and I were scheduled to fly early in the morning and I was to be packed and ready for scheduled transportation at 4:15 a.m. I quickly packed up the one bag I had with me and caught a couple hours of sleep. Then the nurse awakened me and off I went again. At the terminal I found my big bag was missing. I hadn't seen it since Hamilton Field. Then the Captain of the crew reported my black bag had been smashed in lashing down the luggage and all in all I was in a lousy mood.

On the plane they showed me the bag and I was hard put to find the damage. We flew for about fours and then landed at Iwo Jima for about an hour. I took a picture of Suribachi, grabbed some black sand, and then took off in the rain to fly another four hours to Atsugi airport which is approximately 35 miles outside of Tokyo. There I found my brown bag had preceded me.

We drove to Tokyo by way of Yokohama. The things we saw along the road to Yokohama were just like the geography books. Japs working in

Suribachi on Iwo Jima May 16, 1946.

their little fields in water up to their ankles, sometimes up to their knees. I saw all the typical style of houses and costumes. A very young GI riding in with us was just like a kid, he was so excited. Yokohama looked pretty battered and beaten from the little we saw. I reported in at the ATC office in Tokyo and was sent to the billeting office. They put me up at the Old Keijo, formerly a bank, and most recently a male officer billet. I have a certain amount of enemies among the evictees already, they don't like their new quarters as well. At that, they are not deducting anything from our subsistence for our rooms since they don't consider them "livable" as yet. So for the time being it is costing me only 75 cents a day to eat, that is deducted whether I eat there or some other mess, so I can't save money here by being taken out to dinner as I did in Germany. I can hear the howls clear across the Pacific to the effect that I don't have any complaints as is, and I really haven't for in my mind the quarters are much better that I had anticipated.

The place has been fixed up ala hotel style. Since it was just turned over to the girls a month ago, it is still swarming with Jap carpenters. They hammer and pound all day long, but my roommate and I are about one thing, no workee while we are there. They knocked at the door yesterday morning at 9:30 (Sunday) and I told them to go away and stay away. I'd been up pretty late and definitely wasn't in the mood to get up yet, in fact I just made lunch. We have two very nice dining rooms, table cloths, napkins, flowers and very, very polite Jap waitresses, some of whom wear the kimono and sash. I shall need no waist exercises by the time I leave here after responding to all the bows. We can have one guest a meal, I just have to let them know a meal in advance. If aircorps, marine or navy we pay approximately 25 cents.

We have a lounge on the first floor. It's rather barish at present but it is supposed to be improved upon. A bar is in the offing, also a snack bar. I was put into a 3 bed room with two girls who had just arrived by boat. One moved out in a couple days and we were grateful for large as our room is, it still looked a bit cluttered with her trunk, two foot lockers, and six suitcases. She is no glamour puss and considerably older. I would love to know just what all she has in those things.

The most attractive thing about our room is the draperies, of which we have an over-abundance. Windows practically line one side of the room, one regular size and then three together. The side draperies are blueish green lined with lemon yellow. They pull across to serve as shades for night. Then we have white eyelet curtains which can be tied back or left hanging. These have salmon colored draperies behind them which are drawn back or left hanging. They look like a slip under a dress. The eyelet is the kind of stuff which sells for $8 a yard in the States. We all have ideas about evening dresses to blouses so I don't know how long the draperies will last. We badly need bedspreads. I just have army blankets now. But we can't decide which ones to take down for that. Our beds are the regular hospital army style, high built and plain. We each have a good-sized bedside table with a drawer. Some girls have put skirts on these and made dressing tables out of them. Then we have a fairly good-sized oblong table and a small end table, three arm chairs and a rug about 8 x 10. The cupboard arrangement is the built in type, with sliding doors and is adequate for two. I should think it is a bit crowded for three. So far we have no wall plugs, only ceiling lights. That, I hope will soon be remedied.

The Japan maids are all over the place. Three of them go to work on a bed to make it. They chatter like magpies. The head one understands English fairly well. They do our laundry but can't iron worth a darn. My roommate brought an iron so I haven't worried about that yet. There are oodles of little Jap boys at the desk downstairs. One of them looked about 8 years old. He threw my 45 lb. bag up on his shoulder and carried it up to my room. I can't even lift it off the floor. They run up to your room with messages and open doors, always, always bowing. We have two telephones on our floor and if you get a call some girl answers it and comes looking for you. We have shower rooms and lavatories. Whether the other girls take showers regularly or not, I don't know. But I've yet to wait when I want to take a shower or use any of the "facilities". Our meals are attractively served. A typical dinner being tuna fish cocktail, soup, meat and two vegetables, dessert (which sometimes is ice-cream) coffee and of course bread and butter (which sometimes are hot Rolls.)

Of course we have had a couple of meals which were complete wash-outs, but on the whole it is good. Our billet is only two or three blocks from General MacArthur's headquarters and twice as I was walking along the street he has come out of the building. It was almost as though he were watching for me. We traipse around here just as we would at home, at least on the main drags. I'm hesitant about venturing out without male escort but I see other girls doing it. They give you directions at these various offices and send you on your way.

ALLIED GENERAL HEADQUARTERS.

Allied General Headquarters.

I meant this letter to bring you all up to date, but the longer I work on it the longer it becomes. I must get it off today even if I have to leave out stuff. For having been here one week only, they say I have gotten around quite a bit. I've been out to the Peers Club several evenings. It is now an officer's billet and they have a very nice bar lounge, plus a game room off of it. Japanese beer is very good. They say it has a higher alcoholic content than ours, but somehow it doesn't make you feel so full so soon. I believe there isn't as much gas in it. Most places you can get either Japanese beer or stateside beer. Then sometimes we have had Santori (Jap whiskey) or Jap gin, neither of which is half bad. Stateside liquor is far scarcer here than it was in Germany. Maybe I should explain the Peers Club. The Peers of Japan were comparable to the House of Lords in England and this was their social club. It was the most exclusive one in Tokyo, although not the wealthiest. It took blue blood to get in, whereas the Tokyo Club, which was the swank-iest, took money. I haven't been there yet. We have been making ourselves right at home at the other place, playing ping pong, etc. The fellows in our crowd came over with some men who are billeted there, hence our "in".

Last night we opened the officer's club at Palace Heights, a colony of Quonset huts but now a billeting area for single men and transients. It will eventually become the housing area for dependents. This club is quite attractive; in fact the whole set-up ought to be very satisfactory. You should hear the Japs play swing!

Last Saturday night we went to the Red Cross Officer's Club to a dance. That club is in rather a beautiful building, which I understand was built during the war for the Japanese navy officers. They had a good GI orchestra and a floor show of native talent. One exotic dancer did what they announced was a rhumba, if so; they do it differently over here. The first night I was here a Red Cross girl sat at my table for dinner. She was certain that I would be lonesome if I went directly to bed and insisted I come along with her and her date to a Japanese art lecture. I couldn't beg off, even though I was half asleep then. The lecturer appeared at Yale before the war and I suppose knew what he was talking about. I slept.

The next night my roommate (not the heavy luggage gal) introduced me to one of her shipmates and we've been "doing the town". The other night we went down to the Ginza right after I got out of the office.

It is a fascinating place. They have lots of sidewalk shops. The Japs sit on the curb and have these little counters before them. They have everything on earth to sell, their own stuff as well as cameras and other stuff of ours. I understand you have to bargain with them as the first price is usually much too high. It was so late that we just looked and intend to go back to buy. I want some of their "shoes". I really need them for shower shoes. I suspect it will be some job to learn to walk on them. At least one of our girls was having a tough time coming down the hall the other night. We saw some picture book strawberries but of course we daren't eat any of their food. The way it is fertilized causes dysentery and other ailments. The Japs have built up immunity against such diseases. Even seafood is prohibited now because of cholera. These people are so unsanitary and have so much of everything in the way of disease that they have put all Japan theaters and restaurants "off limits" to us. I would have loved to see the Jap theatre. At the office and at our billet we have to get all our drinking water from Lister bags.

I haven't said anything about the general conditions of this city. We did quite a job of bombing. A lot of buildings are still standing, but many are just walls. Quite a number of the downtown buildings, which we have taken over, are very modern. The Dai Ichi building is the very last word. That is where General MacArthur has his offices. The Dispensary and Finances Office are there, too. (This reminds me that the Army pays its travel vouchers right on time, in just one week.) There seems to be more evidence here of fires than there was in Germany. There are coolies and their rickshaws and the GI's keep them busy. Probably about a third of the people still dress in their native costumes, some of which are very colorful. The rest wear anything they can get, it seems. They are a pretty shabby looking people as a whole. When you get off the main streets you find they don't look very well fed. Only those who work for us receive enough food. We were told in orientation that they hadn't had a rice ration for a month. This made me feel very strange indeed to sit down to dinner the other night and have a serving of rice instead of potatoes, especially since I'm not overly fond of it.

There seems to be better organization here about the occupation. So far there has only been one "incident" of Japs ganging up on a couple of GI's and beating them up, whereas we've all heard of the things that happen in Germany. The streets are entirely cleared of rubble here, you don't see the heaps of it in the buildings either. The wreckage in the yards looks more like a junkyard. The Japs haven't many cars, but the streetcars seem to be running pretty well, even to the outer edges of the town. They pack them in until it seems impossible to put another person on. Then they stop at the next stop for more. It is amazing. The trains are operating and I paid my first visit to Tokyo station last night. It was swarming with the natives and I was glad I was not alone, safe though it may be. The trains leave exactly on time. We found that out for the person we were seeing off had to make a flying leap to board it. Military cars are put on and we are supposed to ride in those, although the one last night was an all military train. There doesn't seem to be any place you cannot go provided you have the time. Some of the girls went to NIKKO last weekend and stayed in a Japanese hotel. I guess it was quite an experience, but they said the scenery was beautiful. When you are away from your mess on such a trip you make arrangements with the mess officer before you go and take enough rations to cover the period you will be absent. To do this you have to have authority from your supervisor, even though your absence doesn't interfere with working hours.

They also told us that as soon as we arrive in Japan our names go up on a list and when we are reached in order we automatically become eligible for a trip to a "rest camp" which is in some resort formerly frequented by Americans and Englishmen, hence built and equipped western style.

You are allowed to stay a week and all the customary resort activities are available. You travel on temporary duty orders, so no cost, not even any deduction from annual leave.

4

The Tokyo War Trials Begin

On April 29, 1946, the Chief prosecutor Joseph Keenan was ordered by the tribunal president, Sir William Webb, to serve copies of the Indictment and Charter on each of the accused. The Indictment named the following men.
- Araki, Hata, Itagaki, Minami (former War Ministers)
- Hiranuma, Hirota, Koiso, Tojo, (former Premiers)
- Matsuoka, Shigemitsu, Togo (former Foreign Ministers)
- Nagano, Shimada (former Navy Ministers)
- Doihara, Kimura, Matsui, Muto, Sato, Umezu (former Generals)
- Oshima, Shiratori (former Ambassadors)
- Hoshino, Kaya, Suzuki (former Economic and Financial Leaders)

May 27, 1946 - Dear relatives and friends,

I have been working almost a week now. The International Military Tribunal is now in the War Ministry Building which formerly was the Japanese war college. Our bombers scratched it up somewhat but they are busy hammering and painting all day long. It is about a ten minute drive from the Old Keijo and I have to be out in front at 7:40 (horrible). There are people here from every country, it seems, and it is very interesting in that respect. My own particular job is rather dull at present, but I am told it will not remain so. We have to have a special pass to get into the grounds

Erna at the IMTFE Tokyo Trials.

IMTFE court judges.

and a special mess card for our lunches here. That makes six cards I have to shuffle. I have peeked into the courtroom. What a battery of lights. The trials open June 3rd so we are really putting on steam. I have had a memorandum to the effect that we may be called on to do overtime on very short notice and they do not expect that any 'personal obligations" will interfere. We always work Saturday mornings, and will be working Memorial Day.

IMTFE IPS Team.

IMFTE Trials Japanese defendants (above and right).

Mug shots of Warlords IMTFE.

Japanese warlords entering courtroom for first time

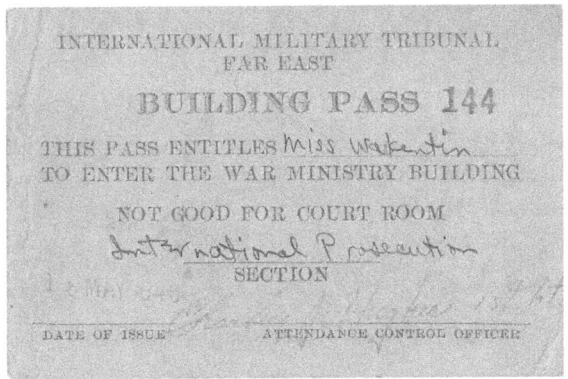

Erna's IMTFE War Ministry Building Pass
International Prosecution Section.

INTERNATIONAL MILITARY TRIBUNAL, FAR EAST
COURT ROOM SEATING DIAGRAM
(READING FROM BALCONY TO STAGE)

DEFENDANTS		JUDGES
BACK ROW	FRONT ROW	
1. ITAGAKI	1. KIMURA	PAL (INDIA)
2. SUZUKI	2. KIDO	
3. SHIRATORI	3. KAYA	ROLING (NETHERLANDS)
4. SHIMADA	4. HOSHINO	McDOUGALL (CANADA)
5. SATO		
		PATRICK (GREAT BRITAIN)
	1. MUTO	HIGGINS *R.J mc+* (U. S. A.)
1. SHIGEMITSU	2. ARAKI	
2. TOGO	3. UMEZU	WEBB (AUSTRALIA)
3. HIRANUMA	4. OKA	MEI (CHINA)
	5. TOJO	
		ZARYANOV (U. S. S. R.)
1. MATSUI	1. MINAMI	BERNARD (FRANCE)
2. OSHIMA	2. HIROTA	
3. NAGANO	3. HATA	NORTHCROFT (NEW ZEALAND)
4. KOISO	4. DOIHARA	JARANILLA (PHILIPPINE)
5. HASHIMOTO		

IMTFE Court Room Seating Diagram.

5

Erna Witnesses History in the Making

June 4, 1946[2] - Dear relatives and friends,

I am not sure I will mail this before I get answers to Chapter I. It just kills me to write two letters to each one I receive. The main purpose of my writing letters being to receive letters. However, I have an excellent opportunity to write now and I may not later and I have the "opening of court" to report on. Today I am pinch-hitting for the fellow who is chief of the investigation division. His secretary is sick. He has been in court all morning and I have been interrupted only twice by telephone calls. I dashed off another run of Chapter I for those I missed on the first go-around and this afternoon I will take up from where I left off. This fellow dashes in once in a while and expresses the hope that I am being kept busy and just to rest if I am not for he will be back later. I keep reassuring him that I have no idle time and everyone else just looks at me banging away and they see the carbon paper sticking out of the machine and assume I am officially occupied. They wouldn't dare to question unless I were reading the paper or some such obvious thing anyway for I sit in the chief's private office and he is their "boss".

Since yesterday's activities are the highlights of this epistle I'll go right into those. Anyway the social activities of last week were not special. I had to work too hard. I worked until 7 o'clock on Memorial Day (Prosecution worked and Defense played yet they asked for more time in Court yesterday), worked all day Saturday and Sunday. I would have played "sick" on Monday, I was so tired, but I couldn't miss the big day. Very conveniently, the capital shift on my typewriter went completely out of order on Monday. I had borrowed a machine for Sunday which had to be returned. So, I found out a way to get passes for Court and got one for AM and PM.

---

2 Erna Warkentin letter June 4, 1946.

Only one other girl from my office got them too and we asked the Captain if we could be excused to attend. I said I only wanted to stay about 15 minutes. He rather hesitated but since he was so rushed himself, before he knew just what was happening I was on my way. Once in, they don't let you leave unless the Court either adjourns or recesses. The first recess came about 11 o'clock. Thinking he would be furious, I dashed out to find my machine still unrepaired, the Captain out of the office so back to Court I went. Supposedly if you leave during a recess you are not allowed to return during that session; however, a smile or two and the MP's make exception for us who work here, at any rate this one did. I left at lunch time and they adjourned till today so I felt very lucky. The Court looks very solemn and is quite a sight. I intend to go back when they are not in session and take a picture of the room, have my signal corps friend develop and blow up the film and then mark it up the way the people sit. All spectators have to be in their seats by 9:15 and Court opened at 9:30.

Half the balcony is for Japanese spectators and the other half for Allied spectators. It isn't too large so the passes are limited. It was interesting to see the Japanese spectators straining for a good look at the defendants. I suspect most of them were members of their families. There are tiers of seats on four sides of the main floor. On one side are Justices, below them their seconds. Sir Archibald Webb (Australian) as president sits in the middle and flanking him are Higgins (U.S.) and Mei (China). Next to Higgins are Patrick (Gr. Britain), McDougal (Canada), Roling (Netherlands) and Pal (India). Next to Mei are Zaryanov (USSR), Bernard (France), Northcroft (New Zealand) and a chair for someone from the Philippines (unoccupied yesterday). Straight across from them are the defendants. Below their box are a couple rows of defense attorneys. The defendants look like a typical bunch of bums brought into court after Saturday night. You can't imagine they are intelligent enough to have caused the trouble they did. It is true that if you look closely there is something sadistic in the mien of some of them. Oshima has the jutting chin and profile of Mussolini and sits there rather arrogantly. Most of them just sit impassively. About half of them were in uniform stripped of all adornment, the others in business suits. Tojo behaved himself and I understand all the fun was taken out of things by removing the fellow who hit him on the head. He is still in the hospital under observation.

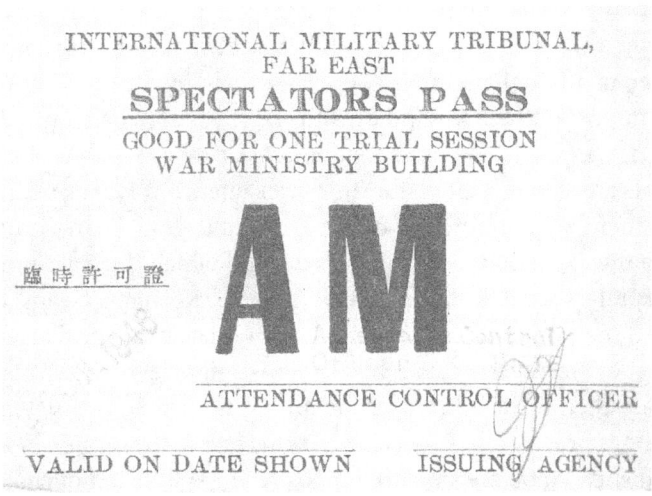

Erna's IMTFE Spectators Pass Trial Session Issued July 22, 1946.

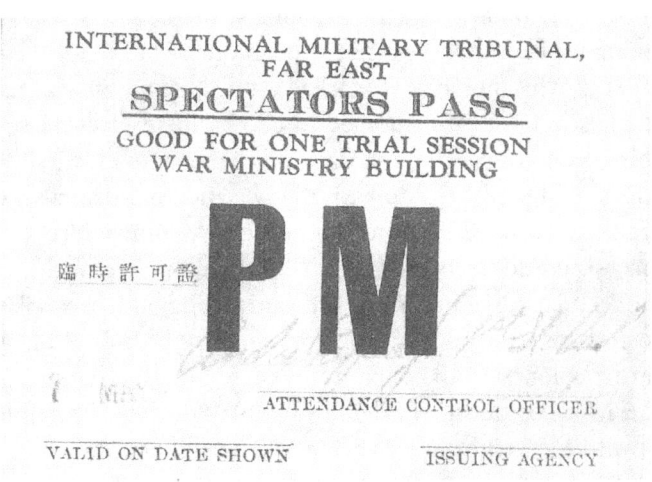

Erna's IMTFE Spectators Pass Trial Session Issued May 7.

They say he really put a spark into the proceedings. Oh yes, the only justice who doesn't wear a black robe is the one from Russia. He is in military uniform. Opposite the balcony are quite a number of tiers of seats, several rows of which are reserved for the prosecuting attorneys and the remainder of the defense attorneys. The other rows above these are for the very important people. Underneath the spectators balcony is the place reserved for newspaper correspondences. Up above the V.I.P's and the defendants are stands built up for the cameramen and every once in a while you hear them whirring away. Could be my picture will be in the newsreels. Down on the main floor are the tables around which the chief prosecutors and interpreters sit. It is at one of these that Mr. Keenan sits, and with him are several men from other countries whom I haven't identified as yet. The table for the interpreters also seats the court reporters. The witness box is just behind them. Just in front of the prosecutors table is the stand where the attorneys present their speeches. At this stand, the witness box, and in front of Justice Webb are small red bulbs. The navy ensign in charge of the interpreters snaps this light on after very few sentences spoken in English and then one of his interpreters translates what has been said into Japanese. When the light is snapped off the speaker can continue in English. Defense pleaded lack of familiarity with the country, the language and the slowness in being processed and asked for postponement (we of the prosecution wondered why they hadn't worked Saturday and Sunday as we did, but since the spectators are enjoined to deport themselves decorously we said nothing.) Of course the first day was taken up with the ironing out of procedural items, what to do with the two men in hospitals, etc. It was finally decided that Mr. Keenan could give his opening address today and then court would adjourn until June 13. I like Sir Archibald Webb. He seems to do a nice job of presiding. Our judge, Higgins seems ok too.

The defendants are brought from prison in a bus. One of our GMC painted army color, with the windows painted blue so no one can look in or out. An MP jeep goes before and one behind, they are painted white and filled with MP's who are well armed. Yesterday after lunch I wandered around to the front of the building and took a chance on my typewriter still being out of commission and waited for the prisoners to leave. I had my camera and a new roll of film. I was the only girl hanging around and about the only camera. That last concerned me a bit for I was afraid pictures were not allowed, but the MP's said they hadn't been so informed.

I took up a position just outside the door, back against a potted tree and set my camera. Promptly at 1:45 the first MP jeep rolled up then the bus and then the other jeep. MP's swarmed the place, bristling with guns. My heart started pounding a mile a minute but I stayed put. Then one of the MP's almost stood in my way and another one punched him to move over a bit so I could have a clear view. They were only two or three feet away from me. Then the prisoners came out. From then on I was busy. I'd take a picture, roll the film, then take another picture, etc. until the roll was finished. I didn't even try to get certain ones. Time was too short. I had several strikes against me. It was a dull day. We were under the portico and my camera might not have been adjusted to the movement, but I took the chance. It seemed worth it. The Lt. Col. MP in charge was very upset because a Jap had somehow got into that part of the courtyard and he angrily ordered that they get him out of there and if any more were allowed in no one would be allowed by that entrance except the MP's and prisoners being escorted into their bus. As soon as they pulled away I dashed inside and up to my office only to find I hadn't been missed. One of the GI's promised to loan me his binoculars if I got a chance to go to Court today and was going to bring them to the door on which he is stationed for me to pick up, but I was sent around here instead. I don't mind missing Court today. I can read Mr. Keenan's speech any time.

Today I am in an office which overlooks the portico. I can see the prisoner's bus parked out here, so when I see it move up, maybe I can dash out and watch the departure without the hampering of picture taking. It is raining today, so I didn't bring my camera. I will finish this page with odds and ends. They have moved a young forest into our lounge at the billets. It consists of approximately fifty potted shrubs, takes away the bareness but seems a little overdone. Tonight I'm going to the 8th Army dance and Thursday night I've been invited to take a boat trip in Yokohama Bay. My date owns a boat. I haven't seen it, but I understand it is a honey.

My roommate and I so definitely dislike our new third bedmate that we are trying to move. To do so, we have to scan a list of available rooms posted on the bulletin board, make a selection and put in a "bid". The room is given to the bidder who has the highest CAF rating and the longest overseas service. Collette's rating isn't as high as mine, but they assured us it would be my rating which would count. We will hear the result tomorrow.

6

Erna Discovers Japan

By virtue of their position, American servicemen had the opportunity to experience the Japanese way of life on a level never before experienced by most Americans, and through such immersion American perceptions of the Japanese people became more refined. American troops found various ways to familiarize themselves with their Japanese counterparts. Some troops did so by getting out of the rubble –filled cities and exploring the Japanese countryside.

Erna in jeep, August 1946.

August 16, 1946[3]

Dear Helena,

I'm so far behind my correspondence; I scarcely know where to start. I guess the best solution would be another carbon copy job, but that won't do for all, but here goes. Japan is still providing a lot of interest for me, I feel there's much still to be seen and done. It's surprising what a difference there is between this occupied territory and that of the ETO (European Theater of Operations). We now work a five day week and most every weekend. I'm off to see another part of the country. I have driven a couple of hundred miles most every weekend lately, and by jeep. Probably the most spectacular thing I tried to do was climb Mt. Fujiyama. I say try advisedly, since I didn't make the top. It has become sort of a fad for everyone to make the attempt.

We had been invited to stay in a Japanese home right on Lake Yamanaka and were to drive the comparatively short distance to the climbing point from there. At the last minute the weather reports came in indicating cloudiness and rain for the weekend so we rather gave up the climb, thinking only to spend the weekend at the lake.

I left my climbing gear in Tokyo and then while driving through the town of Yamanaka in the evening we could see Mt. Fuji so clearly that they started coaxing me to try it after all. I had left all my climbing gear (borrowed) in Tokyo and protested lack of equipment, which was answered by an extra pair of fatigues by one of the fellows and a pair of wool socks by another and an extra sweater. We started later than we originally planned to, beginning the actual climb about 8:30 in the evening, thinking to drive the jeep to station 4. However, the rain had ruined the road below station one and so we climbed from scratch. We stopped at various stations for a cup of tea. The stars were out and it was a beautiful night. We climbed to station 6 by midnight and I was thinking how easy it was compared to the reports I had heard. It continued to be mostly rocks of various sizes. We thought we'd better stop for a bit of sleep and then be at station 7 for the sunrise. I became thoroughly chilled en route not adding anything while resting, so the perspiration from climbing caused the chill. The Japanese "hotel" proved to be a large room with many covered mounds on the floor, which developed to be sleeping Americans. They assured us they had a

---

3 Erna Warkentin letter, August 16, 1946.

better room for our party, better room already housing four more "bodies". They spread out more mats and comforters. I got even more thoroughly chilled for I was constantly trying to keep that darn comforter away from my face. Of course I had perspired a lot climbing and all in all I caught a honey of a cold. We started out again about 3:30 so as to make station 7 for sunrise and at first everything was ok, although that stretch is known as the worst part of the climb and to that I can definitely add my "amen". It was all volcanic slag, very steep and scarcely any path and no vegetation, and very, very steep.

Shinto Worshippers Climbing Mt Fuji, July 3, 1946

We stopped almost at station 7 and watched the sun come up. It was perfectly glorious. However, that stretch did me in, not as far as being tired in my feet and legs. I had congestion in my chest, partly from the cold I had gotten and partly from the altitude, and suddenly every breath I took was a knife stabbing me. I made the station with the help of the guide and my date. We had breakfast there and then I sent the others on. It nearly broke my heart since some of the girls I know have made it, and probably I would have too had we rested there again for several hours. It nearly killed me to stop there, but it probably would have killed me to go on. From where I

34

sat I could see two beautiful lakes, and numerous mountain ridges. I can't honestly say it was worth the tortuous climb, but I'm glad I did it.

They said the scenery, that is the view, was every bit as good from there as farther up and the only thing I missed was the ability to say that I had hit the top. They say only a fool climbs twice or not at all, but we all agreed you must be quite a fool to try it at all, since it is not pretty climbing. The mountain definitely looks more beautiful from a distance. We saw a number of interesting sights, such as the Shinto worshippers who make the trip to the shrine at the top each year as a pilgrimage, they climbed in a file, singing as they climbed and all decked out in big hats and bells, etc. Old people, as well as young were trying to make the trip.

The others came back down around two o'clock in the afternoon and we made the climb down by a little after five. We came down in time to clean up, bid our farewells, and go to the Fuji View Hotel in Yoshida for dinner. That is a resort hotel now used as a rest center for our people and a nicer bunch of fellows couldn't be found who run it. They are GI's. It commands a beautiful view of Fuji across one of the lakes. It is western style. We got there after dinner was supposed to be over, but they arranged for us to eat

Erna Climbing Mt Fuji, July 3, 1946.

anyway, and a quieter bunch of people you never did see. We just wolfed that steak dinner and all the trimmings, and I do mean all, and said nary a word to each other. We left there about ten and it took us until 2:30 to drive back to Tokyo. I was whipped. Have shaken most of the cold by now, but still cough a bit in the mornings. What I do in the line of EXPERIENCE is really something, I think you will agree.

I have a roll of colored film which I am sending home to be developed and I am anxiously awaiting the prints. I have a couple of good "stills" in black and white of the Shinto worshipers climbing and singing as they climbed. It was interesting to watch the faces of the Japanese who make this climb as a pilgrimage to the shrine which is at the top, old people barely able to drag themselves along, and other people carrying babies.

I have been taking in the theatre the last couple of days. Back in the States I would never have thought to enter one during weather as hot as it has been the past month or so, however, not knowing how long I will be here and whether the same performance will be given again I suffered to see. Tuesday night we saw Mikado, given in the most Japanese version it probably ever has been. It was the first time it was presented in Japan since the Japanese always felt it was a take-off on the Emperor and he too holy to allow that. The leading characters were American, but most of the chorus was Japanese girls from the Toho studios, which was comparable

Ernie Pyle Theatre.

to our MGM or some of the other Hollywood studios. I'm afraid the version we are accustomed to seeing is more Chinese than Japanese. The costuming and stage props were excellent. It was given in the Ernie Pyle theatre, which was a leading Japanese theatre before we came in. Unfortunately they have never completed the air-conditioning.

Wednesday was a holiday for us and we took off for Enoshima, an island off the coast of Honshu. It is connected by a footbridge and is literally covered with steps, quaint, narrow streets and has a beautiful view of the Pacific. It has been declared off limits to allied troops as far as the hotels are concerned. All in all we saw no more than a half dozen other allies during the couple of hours we were there. We spent the time roaming over it and looking at the shrines. Then we shopped and bought some odds and ends. By that time we were so hot and dirty we decided to go to the beach near Kamakura (the town where the largest Buddha is). We went swimming for an hour and then started back to Tokyo, about two hours ride. From then on it was hurry, hurry, hurry for I was determined to get to the Imperial Theatre to see the ballet Swan Lake which was being given by the Japanese.

The theatres frequented by the Japanese are off limits to use except on rare occasions when they have one night for allied personnel only. There were no tickets, so seats were given to first come, first serve. Since we finally made it fifteen minutes before curtain time, we got the last row of the highest balcony. At first I thought it was going to be a great disappointment, the dancers seemed so awkward, etc., however, the second act was much better and it grew progressively so. We came to the conclusion that they were all so nervous because of the foreign audience that they weren't doing their best until the applause encouraged them. I will say it was different from the performances I have seen in Washington and London, but I enjoyed it immensely. The theatre was lovely and I'm sure I'll make the next performance when we are again allowed to go in. The costuming and scenery again were excellent.

Tonight we leave for Karuizawa, a mountain resort about five hours drive from here. It was started by an American missionary about sixty-five years ago, a Mr. Shaw, who decided it was a lovely, cool spot as he was traveling across the mountains and came back to start a colony there. A number of people of different nationalities have homes there, many on the western style. Quite a lot of Germans are concentrated there now. It is a virtual

Erna in Enoshima.

Kannan Goddess of Mercy, near Takasaki,
seen on trip to Karuizawa Oct 26, 1946.

concentration camp for them since they are not allowed to leave that prefecture until the authorities decide what is to be done about them. Military Government keeps a pretty close tab on them. We are going to stay in the home of a Canadian woman who is married to a Japanese. She runs a sort of boarding house only as far as we are concerned it is only a rooming house since we bring all our own food and liquids. There are quite a few in our party so it should be fun. We will come back Sunday night. We'll do anything to get away from this Tokyo heat.

I went to church in a very much bombed out Japanese church last Sunday. They had made a temporary altar and the seats were all on uncertain flooring. There was absolutely no ceiling. The minister was Japanese, and the entire service was in Japanese. It was our Episcopalian service.

There were four Americans there, otherwise all Japanese. They gave me an English prayer book so that I could follow the service. They only used one so-called English word, amen, which I concluded must be the same in all languages. Anyway it was a clue to me as to just where in the service we were. It was very interesting.

This will not be one of my book length epistles, but I am so anxious to get a few letters in the mail, that I won't stretch it out any further this time. Court continues to have its interesting moments and I make it a point to sneak in a few minutes each time they put on a different witness. I have seen them all so far.

7

Erna and Japan Life

August 19, 1946[4]

Dear Dorothy,

Almost a month ago I started a long letter to you, which for one reason or another I have just never finished. I seemed to have one spurt of energy and that finished me as far as correspondence is concerned. The other letter is a bit off the beam now in many respects so I'm doing a rewrite.

I continue to manage to make it into Court almost every day. I have seen all the witnesses testify, Rev. Magee on atrocities, Mr. Goette, the INC newspaper man, Mr. Powell, the newspaper man who lost his feet in a prison camp, General Tamaka, Henry Pu-Yi, the boy emperor of China and the puppet emperor of Manchuria, and several others. Of course, I really am not supposed to go in as often as I do, but I have found a place where I can slip in and the powers that be cannot see me. Sometimes it drags a bit, especially when they have a Chinese witness for direct translations are

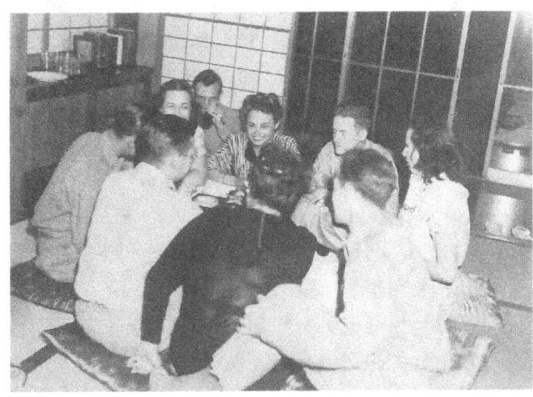

Erna and IPS Staff at Translator House.

---

4 Erna Warkentin letter, August 19, 1946.

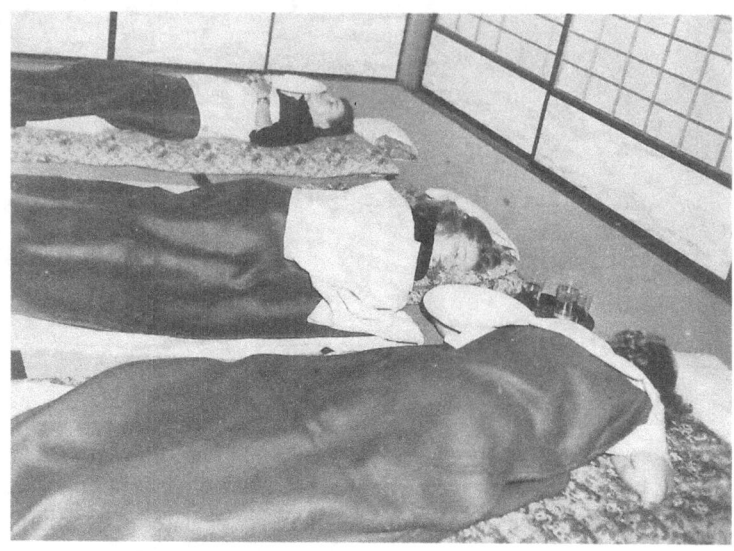

Erna and IPS Staff sleeping at Translator House.

mandatory and each utterance has to be translated, ie, Chinese to English, and Chinese to Japanese, for everyone is afraid of some sense of the thing being lost by Chinese to Japanese to English. Judge William Webb is a hot-tempered person and so is Keenan and they really do battle it out at times.

I received the first package ok, just last week. I've forgotten how you sent it, but most of the girls are having theirs sent first-class. It makes a whale of a difference in the time element. As far as shoes are concerned, the loafers would be most welcome now since I ruined my other play shoes climbing Mt. Fuji. They are at the shoe shop now and it is with fear and trembling that I will go to pick them up. I don't know how they can possibly put them in shape again. I wear that kind of shoe an awful lot when we make these weekend trips. Those and slacks seem to be the prescribed garment. I still am not crazy about them but must admit they are the only thing for trips.

I have a lot of other things, mostly odds and ends and I'll list them here. Do the best you can. I'll asterisk the rush items and I'd appreciate your airmailing those. I can use everything shortly if not immediately.

Combs – grip tooth, little and big*

Lipsticks –Helena Ruberstein, raspberry red and something a bit darker*

White slips – pretty topped for sheer blouses, 31-1/2" short*

Film – 120, black and white and a couple more colored if possible

Thin powder puffs – compact kind

Wash clothes – have stolen two, but should I lose
those, would be bad

Shampoo – Bayve, tube if you can, it comes in both jars and tubes

Sweater – white, long sleeved

Safety pins – large and small

Grip swimming cap – white

Thread – white and black and brown

Household cement – my earrings come off screws and I need it for other
odds and ends

Johnson powder – still prefer it as a talc

Tube cold cream – more convenient for travelling, I can get it in jars here

Triscuits – can always use crackers, which rarely appear in PX's

I will be very glad to get the Nylons. We aren't wearing stockings just
now, but winter is coming and for some strange reason they don't last as
long here. I've gone through practically all I brought. We get one pair a

Int'l Prosecution Section Press Conference Japanese Press Judge McKenzie,
Mr. Sutton, Comdr Guill, Chief Prosecutor Mr. Keenan.

Erna and Office Staff IMTFE Tokyo Trials.

month at the QM, but I never again want to be down to rock bottom as I was in Germany. The ones here of course aren't my best size.

I have been seeing something of a couple of fellows in our office who speak Japanese, having learned it in that army course. IPS (International Prosecutor Section) has a beautiful Japanese home in which they house Japanese witnesses. MP's guard the place and these two officers also live there. I have been out there for a couple of sukiyaki dinners. I have learned to do pretty well with the chopsticks; at any rate I don't go hungry. To add to the atmosphere, the fellows provide kimonos for all, and the Jap maid got quite a kick out of dressing me up in one, obi and all. I'll admit, I prefer my dresses in this warm weather. This is a most unusual house, part of it is oriental and part of it is western and yet it isn't offensive to the eye when one leads into the other. The fellows themselves have one western room and two oriental in their apartment. The fellow who owned the house was very wealthy and hence has some real treasures, but it is different from Germany, one doesn't pick up what one likes over here.

It was one of these fellows who took me to try to find the Nose family. Both Mrs. Brown and Mrs. Everts from Beatrice asked me to forward letters to their old friend. So my friend asked numerous Japanese, we checked the police records for the families in that section, and came to the exact block, but there was no house number such as Mrs. Brown had.

The police have a complete record of every person living in their section, and they didn't have their name at all.

A Japanese person said they had changed lots of house numbers during the war and that might account for there being no house of that number, but the whole neighborhood gathered around our car and none of them had ever heard of the family. The only thing left to do is to have one of our translators write a letter to the folks in Osaka, in third person, telling them he has met me and I have news of friends of theirs which I would like to tell them about and can they get in touch with me in Tokyo. You see, it is still illegal to communicate with the enemy. I had hoped to give the letters to Mrs. Kimura's parents, thinking they would see each other. I hope to go to Kyoto shortly for a weekend and Osaka is a twenty minute trip by train from there.

However, I will still be stymied unless I find someone to take me who knows the language. I have received letters from both Mrs. Brown and Mrs. Everts asking if I found the Nose family, but have not acknowledged them, thinking I would be able to give them real news.   I went to Karuizawa about three weeks ago and also this past weekend. It is about 100 miles from Tokyo, and not especially smooth in a jeep, but it seems worth it to get out of the heat and up into the mountains where it is delightfully cool.

Our rooms in a home ran by a Canadian woman were as neat as a pin, but the kitchen was very primitive. It is a lovely country and the drive up is enjoyable from that standpoint, so I have gotten myself somewhat used to jeep rides and carry on. We were invited to the sea by a Mrs. Azabuchi, the former Japanese woman tennis star. She and her family are the most attractive and most charming Japanese I have met. They have travelled in the States and Europe, their daughter having been educated in Paris. They were instrumental in our being invited to a party at a Count Ito's house, after the local dance was over.

It was some party, whiskey flowed, and they have the most beautiful RCA record player and a beautifully polished floor. Most of the Japanese women were in evening clothes and there were people there of various nationalities. There were five or six other Americans there.

I had better stop this now and get cleaned up a bit, have scrounged (I know you don't like that word) a ride into town to pick up my shoes and go to the PX. Besides, I just got caught writing a personal letter. But

Токуо Р.Х.

Tokyo post exchange.

how I am going to get my correspondence done, I just don't know. I have reread your letters and will make a few comments on the contents; you should see the big brown envelope I carry to work each day.

It gets fatter and fatter with unanswered letters. Your second to the last letter arrived exactly on my birthday, as did one from Hannah and her dad. How is that for timing.

I think this letter is all set to go now. At any rate it is going whether or no. The next one will come sooner and maybe someday I'll get all caught up.

8

Erna and the Japanese Countryside

American servicemen often took their C-rations to Japanese farmers and exchanged them for fresh food items, such as eggs and vegetables. C-rations were highly valued by the Japanese who gladly traded whatever American troops wanted for them. Engaging in trade with ordinary people was an extremely important sign of rebuilding broken relationships. Barriers built up by war propaganda dissipated when both sides encountered each other in everyday settings. US Servicemen in Japan saw the humility of their former enemy because they intermingled with the Japanese people on a daily basis. Seeing those humane qualities bridged the gap between Japanese and Americans and showed that change was possible.

September 9, 1946[5]

Dear Evelyn,

I stayed in Tokyo this weekend and have vowed never again. I get more rest when I go away. I went to a dance Thursday night, Friday night, shopping Saturday afternoon in an art store and record shop and another dance on Saturday night. That dance was over about 1:30 and we had a rendezvous at one of the swimming pools. It was officially closed, but we all climbed the fence. We swam until 3 o'clock. We would really have caught the devil had we been caught by the MP's, but at the time it seemed good fun. There were almost twenty of us, nothing wrong, since we all had stopped to pick up our suits, just was after hours.

Sunday afternoon I drove to Kamakura to see the huge Buddha (2 hours each way), looked over some of the other shrines and drove back in time to have dinner at the new plush GHQ Officer's Club. It was the

---

5 Erna Warkentin letter, September 9, 1946.

Erna in front of Budda Kamakura, July 8, 1946.

entertainment center for Mitsui guests. The Mitsui family is one of the controlling money families of Japan. It is a huge, palatial building, western style, beautiful furnishings, complete china and silver service, tapestry paneled walls, twin fireplaces in each room. Every piece of silver and china, even to the flower vase on the table has their insignia, or should I say crest. The lawn is tremendous and the fountain is set off with colored lights. Last weekend was a long one for us. We had Monday off. I hibernated Monday, Tuesday and Wednesday night. We started early Saturday morning and drove to Lake Chuzinzi which is in the mountains above Nikko. You have to drive over 30 hairpin curves to get there and not being familiar with the road, we postponed going until Saturday morning, instead of Friday after work as we usually do. There is tremendous lake up there and several beautiful waterfalls. We saw them all. We stayed in a Japanese hotel, but went over to the western style hotel for all our meals. The latter is a rest center, but you have to wait until Friday morning to try for reservations there since they never know until then how many of their rest leave people will be on hand for the weekend. I have had some wonderful meals there, candlelight, etc. They have a cable car up the mountain. It looks steep as the dickens, almost like a roller coaster. I vowed I wouldn't go near it, but somehow we found ourselves on the road leading to it and then I was sunk. It wasn't half as bad as it looked. It ran very slowly.

We were going sailing one afternoon, but the weather turned so very cool, the water was choppy, so we had to put that off. The falls are beautiful. It is a sheer drop of water and then runs along over stones which are quite large. You have to take an elevator down through the mountain.

All I could think of was how recently the elevator had been inspected. The water seeped in and dripped on you and the car settled with a bounce on springs in a pool of water. As we were standing on the little bridge

46

Photos from Erna's travels around Japan.

Photos from Erna's travels in the
Japanese countryside.

looking up to the falls, someone pointed out a body on the rocks. There on the rocks was a Japanese who had committed suicide. They said his body had been caught there in the rocks for several days; it looked like a recent thing, the cold water having perfectly preserved his body. Seems people jumping from the top of the falls is one of their favorite suicides.

Am taking every opportunity to travel around and see the country while the weather is good, will take up the concerts, culture studies, and browsing through shops when travelling isn't so favorable. I did do just a bit of that Saturday and brought home a couple of Japanese phonograph records of selections I have liked, also a glass pitcher, looks black but is blue. It's supposed to have been made by the leading Japanese glass artist, a fellow who travelled to Paris, etc. to learn how. I was intrigued by its simple lines and color, not being a connoisseur of glasswork. It cost me over ten dollars. That's the way it will be when I go for this shopping in a big way. There are many "treasures" to buy, but they are not giving them away.

So far the military yen and the native yen are one for one, whereas the prices are pegged at a value of the yen being much cheaper. Military yen are 15 to a dollar; the rate of exchange for the other should be many more yen to the dollar than that. Perhaps if I hold off a bit they will do something about that. There have been numerous complaints so far, however, some of the economists are concerned about increasing the inflationary aspects of the money now. It's a bit involved.

When the cool weather comes I have another project. I have bought a big scrapbook and will go to work on fixing it up. I have taken about a hundred pictures myself and have had others given to me, as well as mementos of other sorts. I know it's best to do it currently, but it is much too warm to do that now. I stay home for an evening to catch up on my chores, sit around just trying to keep cool and vowing to not stay home another evening. It's a rat race.

I am cheating again by writing this at the office. Someone left me their portable so I could do it at home, but that is somehow against my principles. When I come home we will hide ourselves away to some secluded spot and I will tell you of my adventures in greater detail than I can write them.

9

Erna Finds a New Home

September 12 & 19, 1946[6]

Dear Dorothy,

I won't make this a very long letter since I want to catch the mail clerk before he goes in to town after the mail this morning. More of this hard-earned cash for the bank account, in two installments this time. I finally snagged a room to myself. It is huge. I have a bed, two tables, two chairs, one small book case and a large built in closet and a rug. Still, the room looks sort of bare. Maybe it is because I keep it picked up and the closet doors closed, whereas my previous roommate didn't believe in such things. I stayed home Tuesday to catch the carpenters to build racks in the closet and towel racks, etc. and have been puttering around in it in the evenings. I have big ideas of covering the furniture with target cloths and to that end have picked up thumb tacks from the office. My friend Helen also had a single room, and I believe when we get through with them, we will have the most unbarrackslike rooms in the place.

I haven't had the opportunity to go to Kyoto yet, so haven't looked up the Kimura's. However, there was news the other day that we would be allowed to send postcards, so I immediately sent one, giving my address, home and office telephone numbers, and telling them I had "news" of the Browns and Everts and expressing hope that some of them would be in Tokyo soon and could get in touch with me. I imagine Mr. Kimura at least has occasion to come up every now and then. I still hope to get to Kyoto, but it seems a little silly to make that long a trip for a short weekend so I will wait until I can take a couple extra days off. There are a number of places to go from that

---

6 Erna Warkentin letter, September 12 and 19, 1946.

center, including Osaka, and since it is a completely unbombed town the stores are in good shape for shopping.

I can't make this much longer, since I am supposed to be working. Also, having overslept this morning I was an hour late to work. I missed the bus and by the time they got transportation in to me it took that long. I have just managed a single room and it is so quiet compared to the other one that I sleep like a baby. I am fixing it up to suit myself, with knick-knacks, etc.

It is quite large and is only a single because it has only one window but since winter is coming on that doesn't matter at all and I like the privacy, also the ability to decorate as I please. I will write in more detail next time. I want to be sure to get this off this afternoon and I have to walk about two blocks around the building to the mail box.

10

Erna and the China Atrocities

The Rape of Nanking was known to be a deliberate act by Japanese soldiers. It was an incident known around the world and Japan. So the world press widely reported on it during the trial. As the incident was discussed at the trial, one Japanese prisoner in the courtroom, Mamoru Shigemitsu, covered his face in his hands out of shame.

October 23, 1946[7]

Dear Dorothy,

Hope you will be able to make this out without a magnifying glass, it's a borrowed typewriter and since mine is supposed to be back today I refuse to exert the necessary energy to put a new ribbon on this one and my own, too.

Prosecution hasn't finished presenting its case yet, and until it does, I can't make any plans about returning. Even then a staff will have to be maintained and it may be we will all have to serve our year out. It would be nice to be here in the spring for the cherry blossoms, and also there would be that much more money in the bank to splurge with when I return.

However, other than that I will be ready to come home when I can. The man for whom I am working is summing up the China phase of the case, and of course I am thoroughly familiar now with the rape of Nanking and all the atrocities as well as the economic and other phases of the military aggression. What I am working on now will supposedly be used when the prosecution starts to present its closing arguments.

---

7 Erna Warkentin letter, October 23, 1946.

I was invited to a small, informal party given by the Chinese Justice at the Imperial Hotel the other Saturday night. I did a daring thing. One of the Chinese on our staff asked me if I could go. I had another date and said so, but asked if I might bring my date. It wasn't until later I realized I was supposed to be the Chinese fellow's date, but it is just as well. All of these affairs are very interesting and I don't want to miss them, but I'll always prefer to be escorted by one of our fellows. They told me of course I could bring my date and it was something different. They were all Chinese people except for four Americans, and the Justice Mei is a very nice person.

In the next package you send me you can stick in some more of the medium size combs if you have been around to the dime store. My hair is so thick on the sides that they do fall out. You see your hair gets blown about more in a jeep than a sedan but then you wouldn't know that, would you?

Really did appreciate the book review sections you sent me, although it made me realize how far behind the times I am on what is bring published these days for I recognized all too few titles amongst the best-sellers. This letter can be the one to authorize the sending of those New Yorkers, which I'd love to have. They don't sell it in the overseas editions here as they did in the ETO. Time, Newsweek and Reader's Digest are the only magazines our PX's carry. Which reminds me, someone told me that an issue of Life sometime back carried pictures (colored, I believe) of the Mikado as it was presented at the Ernie Pyle Theatre here. If you still have that copy, would you please either send me those pictures or save them for me?

I expect it must seem to you that I'm requesting a lot more clothes than I did when I was in the ETO, but the situation is different here than I anticipated and far different from the ETO. Tokyo is swarming with both civilian girls and dependent wives, all bringing over the latest and best, and no one dresses down as we tried to do for the sake of the English women. The terrain, namely the beaten up streets, are rough on shoes, which don't seem to be made as well as pre-war in the first place.

I wrote you about sending the card to the Kimura's. It took almost three weeks for them to receive it and just today I received their answer, which took over two weeks to come to me. Helen and I were planning, finally, on making the trip down to that territory weekend after the coming one. But when I put in my request for orders twelve days in advance, as I had been told to do by my section, I was informed that so many people are going to

Kyoto (which is the place I would have to go for billeting and transportation and then find my own way to Osaka), that all weekend reservations are filled until after Armistice Day. We will keep our fingers crossed for cancellations on the other.

That will make Christmas presents late too, for everyone who has been there tells me that that is the place to spend your money and get the best quality, even though the cost may be a bit more. I will do the best I can on your $10, but I may have to go a bit higher or put that in with my Christmas gesture, for again the native merchant has spotted the GI and the prices are a great deal higher than they were before the war. The people who lived here back then all say the same thing about that. The official exchange is 15 yen to a dollar, whereas the market is way above that.

As you can well imagine, there is a great deal of money exchanged outside of the Finance Office. The Japanese peg their prices on the market rate, whereas military government refuses to sanction more than 15 to a dollar. They (Economic section of SCAP) says if they change it it will be conducive to inflation more so than is presently true; but certainly they aren't getting anywhere this way. It is very simple to find someone who will exchange military script (we get it in dollar denominations now) for the old yen which you use in Japanese shops, and at the rate of at least twice and mostly three times the Finance Office rate. It is common knowledge, too.

Last Sunday I attended church at the Meiji Building, which is the PACUSA headquarters. The chaplain was asking for offerings to further the activities here, and with a smile made the comment that he understood most of the fellows had plenty of old yen and since he had to use that anyway, they could put either one into the offering plate.

The boss is back from lunch now, and while I spent all afternoon typing his personal letters, I suspect he thinks that I should now be working on his brief, so I'll just copy in the postcard on this page and sign off.

I received the following letter from the Kimuras's.

Oct. 7th, 1946 – Osaka[8]

Dear Miss Warkentin

I am exceedingly delighted to have received today your card of Sept. 18 and much appreciate your concern at our welfare and so much troubles you have taken in trying to find the Noses. It is a great comfort and delight to us to learn that the Browns and Everts are thinking of us so much as to have given you messages to us and that they seem to be getting along fine. I and my wife wrote some time ago to the Browns at Lakewood and the Everts at their store and are hoping our cards will find them all right. My eldest son, Michio, will be in Tokyo shortly to study at a college and will have the pleasure of seeing you just as soon as he settles down there, when he will tell you all about us. We shall be much pleased if you will see us when you will come down here which we sincerely hope will materialize soon.

—S. Kimura

---

8 S. Kimura letter, October 7, 1946.

11

A New Constitution in Japan

During the Occupation, Japan adopted a new constitution (sometimes called the MacArthur Constitution because of the major role Americans played in its drafting). This constitution was completely different from the Meiji Constitution of 1889.

- The biggest change was that it declared that sovereignty rested with the people, not the emperor. This is the political basis of democracy.

- The emperor was to continue as a symbol of Japanese unity and culture, somewhat like the Queen of England in Britain's democracy, but without any political authority whatsoever.

- The supreme political institution was now to be Japan's parliament, the Diet, which was to be made up of freely elected representatives of the people.

- Women were given equal rights under the new constitution, including the right to vote.

- Local governments were strengthened to encourage "grass-roots level" political participation.

- The constitution established many new civil liberties, such as the right of free speech, and the powers of the police were weakened and carefully regulated.

- Finally, the military forces were completely abolished and Article 9 of the new constitution forbade Japan to maintain an army or go to war ever again.

November 3, 1946[9]

Last Sunday the Japanese celebrated the promulgation of their new Constitution. It was quite an affair.

I went over about 11:30 to take pictures of the crowd. I took miscellaneous shots of girls in pretty kimonos, guards, etc. They had a tremendous stand built on the Imperial Plaza. All fastened with bunting, etc. Quite a crowd had already gathered. The streets were crowded with people headed that way. I thought perhaps some part of the program was going to be given then, but found out that the celebration started at 2 o'clock and that the Emperor was to appear. Back I went at 2. It was only about three blocks from my billet, but this time I took someone with me.

We climbed a truck and took a picture of the crowd, we climbed on the platform and took pictures of the dignitaries all standing there in their swallow-tail and boutonnieres, in fact got quite close to them, then we lined ourselves up with some more Americans along the pathway where the Emperor would come to reach the platform.

About 2:30 he arrived in the State carriage. It was all red and gold and black. Then I was so excited I'm not sure what kind of picture I got, everyone had only about two films left and wanted to get the very best shot, besides being excited too, so we all got in each other's way. He looked like a very meek little man. The Empress is sweet looking but rather matronly and not petite as so many of the aristocratic women are. The Japanese really worship the Emperor and shouted "Bonzai" again and again.

When he had passed we went up to behind the people who were to release the pigeons as the Emperor greeted the gathering. He only appeared for two minutes, so we turned to go back to the path again and everything was very much under control. I was right on the front line, this time with no film and just to concentrate on what I could see. All of a sudden, without the slightest warning, an avalanche descended on me. I can't explain it any better. The Japanese simply lost all control and stampeded forward to get a better look or just to be close. It was the most fanatical demonstration I ever hope to see or be involved in. I don't know yet how I ever came out alive.

There wasn't a thing you could do. You were swept along with the mob. The only thing that saved us was that some of our people were hanging

---

9 Erna Warkentin letter, November 3, 1946.

onto a lamp post, they reached out and grabbed one of us and that one grabbed me and we hung for dear life. All this time I had my camera under my arm. Not yet put away in the case and was clutching the roll of film I had removed and which I hadn't been able to seal since the sticky paper was glued to the film roll.

I somehow managed to hang on to both and hope and pray I didn't expose my pictures. When the Emperor's carriage drove off, the crowd broke up, and we headed for home, every bone in our bodies aching. The next time I go to see the Emperor it will be as a result of a personal invitation to the palace and thus no effort required on my part. It gave me an idea of how they got the people to fight the war and what made them drive insanely onward.

Erna at Constitution Day, 1946.

Erna at Constitution Day, 1946.

Emperor Hirohito on stage at Constitution Day, 1946.

Emperor Hirohito in a carriage at Constitution Day, 1946.

(Above and below) Emperor Hirohito walking
during Constitution Day, 1946.

Erna far right with camera taking photo of Emperor Hirohito.

12

Erna Escapes Death in Hokkaido[10]

Here is another brief chapter in my experiences over here. I'll try to give you a report on both my long weekends, which followed one another and consequently put me way behind on letters and other personal duties. I even worked three evenings to catch up on stuff at the office.

First, the weekend after Armistice Day our orders at last came through for Kyoto. It is an overnight's trip on the train, much too far to drive considering the condition of the roads over here. As you probably know, it is the cultural center of Japan and was not touched by the war. Nara, approximately two hours by train from Kyoto, was the first capital of Japan and Kyoto the second, hence there is a world of history in this territory. There are cloisonné factories, lacquer factories, pottery, silk, etc. as well as numerous shrines and temples.

Since I wanted to visit some Japanese people, I asked for an extra day of annual leave, planning to make that visit on Monday and do the usual tourists trips and shopping on Saturday and Sunday.

However, these people asked me for Sunday so that was when I went to see them. We arrived in Kyoto early in the morning and after breakfast went on a shopping tour.

I am not keen about organized tours, but we felt it was the quickest way to get ourselves acquainted with the shops. We visited several places where they showed us how lacquer work is done, and how cloisonné and pottery is finished. I didn't buy too much, but did find some lovely things.

Inflation has caused everything to be much higher than it was before the war. We returned to the hotel in time for lunch. There was a factory tour just after lunch and since I had never visited a silk mill, I decided that was a good idea and went along. It was most interesting. We also visited

---

10 Erna Warkentin letter, November 1946.

display rooms of beautiful tapestries, and obie cloth, none of which were for sale. Pure silk cannot be sold by the Japanese under SCAP (Supreme Commander of the Allied Powers) orders. We are able to buy some now and then through the PX (Post Exchange). One of my friends had a letter of introduction to a pottery place and we visited this man's private collection and he had tea served to us in a modified tea ceremony. It's quite a rite. There's even a special way to pick up and hold the cup, etc., a special room for it is to be served in and certain motions in the preparation of the tea.

The next morning the Japanese man (a friend of Tex's folks, who with his family lived in Dallas for many years) came after me at the hotel and took me to his house where all the family had gathered to meet me. They were pitifully grateful to see someone who knew their very dear friends whom they hadn't seen for so long and hadn't even heard from for over five years. They served me a wonderful Japanese dinner and gave me a kimono they had had for over 20 years. It was a most interesting day.

The next day I had a wonderful opportunity to go by train to Nara. We had thought of getting a jeep to drive around in when we arrived there, but instead took rickshaws (two wheel cart pulled by a runner). I have wanted to ride in one for a long time, but never had the courage to in Tokyo since I thought I would feel so conspicuous. However, Monday is not a tourist day in Nara and I don't suppose there were another dozen people around, none of whom I knew. It was a beautiful, sunshiny day and we rented the things for three hours. Nara Park is quite large and there are many shrines and temples in it. Our pullers would just wait for us and we went in everywhere and took our time looking and taking pictures. The biggest Buddha in the world is in one of the buildings and it is simply tremendous.

There is one particular shrine which has two thousand stone lanterns leading up to it, each lantern is between five and six feet high. There are also a thousand metal hanging lanterns. There are deer running free in the park and it is all overlooked by a mountain which they also consider sacred.

As you can see, I was on the go the entire three days, and what with going to a dance on Saturday night and a party on Sunday night; I was very much on the tired side when I caught the evening train on Monday to come back to Tokyo. I arrived in Tokyo to report to work at 9:30 on Tuesday morning, just an hour and a half later that I was supposed to and worked Tuesday, Wednesday and Thursday. On Friday morning three of us girls took off on the courier plane to fly to Hokkaido, the island north of Honshu where we are stationed. We were supposed to take off at 8 in the morning and finally did at 11. We dropped down in Sendai for lunch and arrived at Chitose airfield around 3:30.

From there it is a drive of over an hour into Sapporo where we had made arrangements to stay. It was cold and clear up there and on Sunday we had snow. It is a country more like some we know at home, the first cattle I have seen, other than in the zoo here in Tokyo, and the crops are more like ours. They also have more buildings like our houses. We went shopping and bought some wooden carvings of Hokkaido bears and also took lots of pictures. Had some very good times with the Americans stationed up there and had my first real shrimp, simply huge.

We wanted to take the train back to see all the scenery en route and when we heard the plane we flew up on crashed on its return trip that made it positive. We arranged reservations, even though we didn't have the necessary official orders and left on Sunday night. It is a 36 hour train trip, but very comfortable. We had compartments and the meals were very good. We girls are not allowed to travel on the trains on overnight trips unless we have Pullmans or compartments, and of course, must travel on trains especially reserved for allied personnel. It was a very interesting trip, it takes five hours to cross the channel and they just load the whole train on the ferry.

Just off the coast of Hokkaido we all had to dress and go up on deck since they think there are still mines floating in the waters up there and take all precautions. It was a wee bit early, five o'clock, but I think it was worth it for the sunrise over the water was beautiful. Of course we stayed out on the open deck as much as possible so as to see everything we could. I have said it before and will say it again; there is magnificent scenery over here.

We got back early the next morning and again I reported to work on Tuesday. My boss was so alarmed by what happened to the plane so soon after we got off of it, that he forgot all about my being gone an extra day. We timed it just right, for now no one can fly any more unless they have official business.

What with winter setting in, and so many restrictions put down, my trips will almost be a thing of the past here. Armistice Day weekend they spoiled many plans by putting all Japanese hotels "off limits". Since there are far more of us over here than the approved Army rest centers can

GENERAL HEADQUARTERS
SUPREME COMMANDER FOR THE ALLIED POWERS
INTERNATIONAL PROSECUTION SECTION

APO 500
14 November 1946

SUBJECT: Transportation to Sapporo, Hokkaido

TO   : Transportation Officer, ATC.

    1. The following-named employees of the International Prosecution Section, GHQ, SCAP, have obtained permission to be absent from their duties ~~from their duties~~ from 0800 hours, 22 November 1946, to 0800 hours, 25 November 1946, and desire to visit Sapporo, Hokkaido, during that period:

        MISS ERNA WARKENTIN
        MISS MARY A. FRIEDMAN
        MISS WILLIANNA SETTLE

    2. If it is at all possible, it will be appreciated if air transportation can be furnished for these people.

THEODORE GOULSBY
Lt. Col., Cav.
Executive Officer

Erna's Transportation Orders to Sapporo, Hokkaido, November 1946.

The Hokkaido ferry.

Erna and 347th Harbor Craft Co.

accommodate, it means more weekends in Tokyo. I don't mind too much for I will now settle down to getting packages off, letters written and my own room straightened up. I did feel, though, that I should take in every opportunity to travel as much as I could.

Maybe you will be interested in Thanksgiving Day. Maybe it would be kinder not to tell you about all the wonderful food we had, since news from the States indicates that things are pretty hard to get. We had a complete dinner at the place where I live. So much I couldn't eat it all. Turkey, dressing, etc. and mince meat pie, pumpkin pie and ice cream.

I went to the football game in the afternoon. Seems strange to think last Thanksgiving I went to one in Frankfurt, Germany. In the evening I went out to dinner and had the same thing all over again. Every billet in town had free, stateside liquor all day, so you can imagine it was quite a celebration. In case you think I forgot, I did get to church in the morning!

I must get back to work now. As you can well imagine, I am behind here, too. I grabbed the opportunity to type these two pages while I was alone. I can tell so much more that way than writing by longhand. Even so, if I were to sit down and talk to you I could tell you even in greater detail of all the things I have seen and done but that will have to wait a bit. Must stop now and walk about two blocks around the building to get this in this morning's mail, and then to work. Had hoped to go away this week, but we are much too busy and amazingly enough the Judges decided not to recess for the holidays.

13

Christmas in Japan

December 27, 1946[11]
Ashiya, Japan

Dear Miss Warkentin,

Thank you very much for all of those presents you kindly sent us. It was so nice of you to send us so many lovely things. Mimi came back home the day before X'mas and I am so glad to learn from him that you are in excellent health. We all were surprised and delighted at finding on X'mas day so many very nice X'mas presents you so kindly gave all of us, which Mimi deliberately concealed from us until X'mas morning to surprise us, and which added so much to the gay atmosphere at our X'mas celebration. There on the table we found so many packages of presents and a Christmas cake. From the packages came so many wonderful things one after the other that we could not guess where they came from. I think we had to believe in Santa Claus only for this time. Each of them was what we needed most. How delicious was the Christmas cake! We certainly did have a Merry Merry Christmas and thank you heartily. We all hope you come visit us again. Mimi will go back to school the middle of next month and will tell you all about us. We wish you a very Happy New Year.

Love, Miyoko Kimira

---

11 Miyoko Kimura letter, December 27, 1946.

January 6, 1947[12]

Dear Dorothy,

Yes, things have changed and here I am again batting out a letter on this old thing at home. Not only am I busy as the dickens at the office, but I spend all my spare energy there in just trying to keep warm. They turn on the heat for about an hour at a time twice a day, and today not at all till after lunch. The only thing that keeps me there at all is the fact that I am on the side of the building which benefits most by the sun and my desk is right up against the window. They say there is a shortage of coal. Today we heard the last shipment was half sand. Be that as it may, my room here is so warm that if I want to get anything done before I fall asleep I have to keep the door open and turn off the heat. I loan out my room to other girls in the building whose radiators don't work so well. They have to get out when I come home to sleep. This is a far cry from the office where I work with my coat on lots of times and most of the girls wear their wool slacks.

I have my room fixed up fine now. I have a special service radio which works fine now that I have a transformer to adjust the current. Jap current is too weak for the powerful set I have. I can get the States on it.

We get all kinds of snack food at the at the PX (post exchange) now and occasionally crackers, can always order cokes and beer, Suntory whiskey and our Stateside liquor rations have been coming in pretty regularly now. I bought one, $20, consisting of about six bottles of whiskey, two of gin, one brandy, one rum, and we can send the hall girls down for ice. I have a thermos I can get filled with coffee, and several of the girls have hot plates and can make coffee.

I always seem to know someone with a commissary card so I can get coffee that way, too. The only time I haven't had maid service was on New Year's Day, which was a super holiday for the Japanese and they let the room girls have the day off. I only wash my nylons because I figure the girls will snag them all to pieces. They even iron my blouses, etc. I haven't found one to mend for me yet, but they have a dressmaker downstairs. In fact, two such shops. Sounds like a lazy life doesn't it? My boss has it even easier. He dictates his letters. Our only drawback is that we can't

---

12 Erna Warkentin letter, January 6, 1947.

have men above the first floor so you can only have hen parties and can't return hospitality. There's no place, for instance, where I can entertain the Kimuras.

I don't know why I did all that rambling above, when there are certain things I especially want to write and I am sukoshi (Japanese for a little weary.)

Have lots of good reading material now. All those magazines you sent plus three books from Evelyn, Sholem Asch's East River, Inglis Fletcher's Toll of the Brave and Ferril's I Hate Thursday. Have read over half of East River and parts of I hate Thursday. Have you read any of them? Want also to go back to seeing how much I can get out of this travel book of Japan which I picked up in Karuizawa which is in German. Incidentally I am now studying German at school. I finished the philosophy class. Other powers that be decided to purge the teacher. They found he was trying to inject undemocratic and other Japanese political ideas into his lectures. It wasn't so bad for the evening classes for they were old enough to question his statements, but too many G.I.'s were swallowing it whole cloth. They found he was a member of a society which was purged early in the occupation. The people I meet!

I sent a big bag to the Kimura's when Mimi went down for Christmas. Incidentally, I didn't make a carbon of the letters I wrote you about that trip and when I read your letter I decided if it was that good I'd better hurry and write to see if you would save it for me. You see I've been trying to keep carbons to have some kind of a record of my adventures.

Back to the Kimuras's, I sent a lot of my cotton clothes and some odds and ends of food, the large fruit cake and some compacts for the girls. I had a card yesterday from Mr. Kimura. Evidently one of their friends delivered it by hand here to the hotel. He said Mimi had carefully hidden the things and hadn't brought them out until Christmas day! That Mimi is quite a lad. He got tickets again to take me to the Kabuki plays. I told him Ok, but that if the MP's were floating around I might have to do a little fancy talking and so we went. No one was around, but I did feel very conspicuous for I was the only white- skinned person present. Naturally, his explanations, in English, and my answers attracted the attention of all our neighbors. I had a funny feeling. He had gone to the theater several days before and had bought a program and had translated the cast of characters and the synopsis for me. He had it all carefully written out.

Probably there are other things I should write, but it is past ten now and I think that tomorrow I ought to allow myself more than ten minutes to dress, which is what I had today, nicht wahr? My next letter, I hope, will tell you of plans for trips I am cooking up.

I'm not sure why I held this letter up for my activities over the holidays were nothing out of the ordinary. On Christmas Eve I broke up the party by insisting on going to church. Episcopal services were held in the Imperial Theater which had absolutely no heat. Other people went with us and since they have all been asking whose idea it was that we go there and freeze for two hours. Had tickets to go to some special performance being held there one Sunday afternoon and when I suggested it to the fellow with whom I had a date he said he would take me there but after Christmas Eve. No amount of devotion to me would drag him inside. Anyway, I did get to church.

We didn't work the afternoon before Christmas and had a big cocktail party thrown by some of the IPS crowd. The Chinese Division was the only one not represented. The Russians were there en masse. One of the girls asked one of the Russians here for dinner on Christmas Day and he had to turn it down. They are never allowed to go anywhere alone. And she thought she would show him a nice Christian holiday!

Erna having dinner with the Russians.

Went out again on Christmas Day, dancing and drinking, but I saved my real howling for New Year's. I started that out with a buffet dinner and on to several spots and back to the same apartment to eat again before calling it a night.

Went out to a dinner party the next day at noon and to a cocktail party and out again in the evening.

New Year's Eve I wore my black formal, other times the dress you sent me and it made a tremendous hit. At the Mitsui Club I overheard several people comment as I went to the dance floor "Isn't that a pretty dress?" I must really end this now.

14

The Prosecution Concludes Their Evidence

January 25, 1947[13]

Dear Miss Warkentin,

Yesterday we concluded the Prosecution's evidence. In the more than six months since the trial began we have not requested a moment's delay for production of a document or a witness in spite of the terrific language and processing problems involved. This is an all-time record and is unparalleled in the history of legal jurisprudence. All who have participated in this unique accomplishment have a just reason to be proud.

The problems were particularly difficult during the last thirty days of the trial, and the maintaining of our record during this period was, to a considerable extent, made possible by the efficient and capable attention you gave to the execution of your assignments.

The initiative you displayed in withdrawing documents from the processing pool and setting up an organization in my office for supplementing the work of the processing departments, thereby enabling us to meet deadlines, is worthy of special commendation.

I also want to take this opportunity to thank you for the splendid manner in which you have carried on the complicated work of my office.

Sincerely,
Frank S. Tavenner Jr.

---

13 Frank S. Tavenner Jr. letter, January 25, 1947.

GENERAL HEADQUARTERS
SUPREME COMMANDER FOR THE ALLIED POWERS
INTERNATIONAL PROSECUTION SECTION

25 January 1947

Dear Miss Warkentin,

Yesterday we concluded the Prosecution's evidence. In the more than six months since the trial began we have not requested a moment's delay for production of a document or a witness in spite of the terrific language and processing problems involved. This is an all-time record and is unparalleled in the history of legal jurisprudence. All who have participated in this unique accomplishment have a just reason to be proud.

The problems were particularly difficult during the last thirty days of the trial, and the maintaining of our record during this period was, to a considerable extent, made possible by the efficient and capable attention you gave to the execution of your assignments.

The initiative you displayed in withdrawing documents from the processing pool and setting up an organization in my office for supplementing the work of the processing department, thereby enabling us to meet deadlines, is worthy of special commendation. I also want to take this opportunity to thank you for the splendid manner in which you have carried on the complicated work of my office.

Sincerely yours,

Frank S. Tavenner Jr.

FST-ib

Acting Chief Prosecutor IPS Frank Tavenner Jr. letter.

15

A Death at the Office

January 27, 1947[14]

Dear Dorothy,

Life has been rather hectic here the past three weeks and this letter won't contain much in the way of adventures in Japan in the sightseeing sense of the word....but...

First of all, with my boss Frank Tavenner in charge of the last part of the evidence introduced by Prosecution, you can imagine that we've been working at a terrific pace. I worked weekend before last, both days, the other girl I have in the office now worked the next weekend and I was slated to work this past Saturday and Sunday. In addition to this full-time girl we had another girl part time and also a man. Our work consisted of a lot of follow-up, checking, cutting red tape and doing other people's work in order to meet deadlines.

Friday morning I was still working on something which was rush, and Louise had just gone into the next office and brought me a cup of coffee, when someone burst into the office telling us to get Tavenner immediately, McKinley was sick in the hall.

McKinley's desk was just three feet away from mine. We tore out to find that he had dropped unconscious in the hall, and when we got to him his face already was a deep purple and he was barely breathing.

He married one of the secretaries over here in October. I believe Sutton told you about that. She had just passed him in the hall five minutes before. They had her and of course she was practically in hysterics.

---

14 Erna Warkentin letter, January 27, 1947.

We girls took care of her in the ladies lounge until the doctor came to tell her it was all over. They said it was a heart attack. Part of the time I was alone with her and I would be so thankful when she started to be quiet until she seemed to be so quiet she was becoming unconscious and then that would worry me. It was quite an ordeal since we had to keep her thinking there was still hope until the doctor came. As you can imagine, it was almost the straw that broke the camel's back. Almost half the afternoon was spent making arrangements and Louise went home to Mac's wife's billet with her. Saturday we started to work out at the house and Mr. Higgin's brought the girls out for lunch. The atmosphere was rather strained. Then the hospital called and I had some calls to make and call them back and in struggling with these ***********ad infinitum, Japanese telephones I did just about go to pieces. Thank heavens, Tavenner decided that in view of everything we wouldn't work Sunday. Today I had to get all the personal things out of Mac's desk, (this is a new typewriter, as you can see, but I hope you will appreciate that I do try to write letters, even when I am out on a date.)

Last Tuesday I had an urgent call from one of my friends in town, telling me that the main boiler at my billet had blown up and that there would be no heat or hot water for at least ten days and maybe much longer. All the girls were being moved into other billets. That called for a hurried trip into town to arrange that I be moved (I was interrupted right there by a bid of a medium rare steak, our steaks here are usually cooked to a crisp), to another billet. I'll skip all the furious mix-ups, etc., and just say I did get myself moved that evening. Indications were that it might be for several weeks, but when I came home last night I found that the last meal served in the new hotel would be Saturday afternoon, and since I'm keeping my fingers crossed on going away for the weekend, that means I have to be moved back by Thursday night, not even ten days.

As you can see, I'm almost inclined to agree with Sutton. I seem to have the faculty of always being where things are happening, but the above two happenings I would have much preferred not to be involved in. Sutton arrived back in town Sunday and everyone, including Sutton, is wondering what happens to me next. Tavenner is letting it ride with the excuse that he didn't say <u>when</u> he would let me go back. Sutton reminded Tavenner of his promise by letter just before he left the States.

By now you have probably received a tubular package containing paintings on oil silk. They are not (repeat not) your Christmas present, only some more of my loot sent to you for safekeeping. I suggest you get back that wooden box and rent a locker at a storage place. There is another box on the way in addition to the box I wrote you about. Would you be so kind as to itemize the contents of the boxes if they appear at all damaged or repacked? I have them all insured. One of the girls received word that her packages has been horribly mistreated, contents broken and missing.

We had another earthquake during the funeral services this morning. It was slight, not nearly as bad as the one which caused so much damage down south.

I am working tonight. We have a new girl to take Louise's place since Louise has been "assigned" to taking care of McKinney's wife in getting her and her personal belongings ready to take the plane home on Thursday. Tavenner was going to have the new girl work, but I had heard her break a date after she was asked to work and I was afraid she would get stuck and have to stay beyond the time she had told her date she would be home. Louise says I keep her happy by peeling tangerines for her. What you won't do to keep the staff happy!!

This will be all the rambling for now. In order that there be no confusion perhaps I'd best say that your Christmas present is the box which contains one item only. If this letter doesn't sound too cheerful, please make allowance this time. I must confess that by Saturday afternoon I had a bad case of nerves.

16

The Kimuras Put Erna at Risk

February 7, 1947[15]

Dear Dorothy,

The boss decided to take a weekend in Kyoto so Louise and I are catching up with your personal mail. I wrote letters yesterday and am doing so again today until noon when I will take off for town. Louise is off this morning. We just look past the work very quickly. The files are in bad shape, but my envelope of unanswered letters I figured was in worse condition.

We have been working out at the house quite a lot lately as there we have much fewer interruptions. Day before yesterday Louise and I said we were going for a walk for about fifteen minutes right after lunch. Of course the neighborhood around Mitsui House (where Keenan, Higgins and Tavenner live) is strange to us and before we knew it were hopelessly lost, and ended up in the other direction from the house from which we started, and almost two hours later. By the help of Japanese policemen and a Japanese man dressed in pin-stripe trousers and cutaway coat, and finally in a GI truck, we got back just as Mr. Tavenner was going to send the driver and his car to scout the neighborhood for us for he realized then that we must have gotten ourselves lost.

We had a marvelous time though, prowling through Japanese formal gardens, past lumber mills, down alley-like streets where probably no white person has been since the occupation, past the Tokyo institution for the blind, etc. etc., climbed through fences and up down hills. The GI we saw on the way back, after we finally got a Jap policeman to draw a map for us, was the one and only American we saw the entire time.

---

15 Erna Warkentin letter, February 7, 1947.

Still haven't heard from Mimi, and since I am almost incommunicado at the new billet and haven't been working at the office for the greater part of the past two weeks, I guess I'd better write him a note and ask him to come around at a certain time. Have only received the candy but do want to get it to him. Mrs. Brown wrote asking if I was getting into any trouble being the middle man. Of course I'm doing what I'm not supposed to be doing but the authorities blink at it if it is done in such a small way. However, I could have shook Mr. Kimura when I read in her letter that he had told them of my visit and how much they appreciated the letters I brought!! I have written Mrs. Brown and will surely remind the Kimura's that correspondence on things I deliver is taboo, but definitely. The folks back in Texas will just have to assume the Kimura's appreciate the gifts and the Kimura's will just have to forego expressing their appreciation until later.

I have a chance to go to Atami tomorrow morning. It isn't under the usual circumstances I have taken trips, but we all feel it will be worthwhile. Practically ever since I have been here that area has been off limits, with the exception of a rest center for enlisted men. The officer in charge has asked one of my friends to bring a group of girls down for the dance Saturday night, that time being the only time we are obligated to spend with the youngsters and at the same time all the accommodations of the hotel are ours. Since it is the only way we can figure out to ever get there, we are going, at least eight girls I know well, we leave on the ten o'clock train and I will return Sunday afternoon.

The 18th of February I leave for a week of annual leave at the resort in the Japanese Alps, Akakura. If next you hear of me with a broken leg do not be too surprised for they say that inevitably you do get on the skis up there, oh, me. It is the only place we can visit now other than a hotel which is accessible for weekends and I couldn't see the point in that. Me, I want to see something new.

Prosecution rested its case week before last, and the motions to dismiss were set aside and court adjourned this Monday. We are now in a three week recess. Tavenner finally took the bull by the horns and arranged for another girl to work for Sutton, which I understand didn't make Sutton too happy, but he admitted it made sense since I knew this work now and he would be starting out on a new tangent.

I hardly knew how to lean my weight. Tavenner is higher up on the ladder and for that reason I know more of what makes the wheels go around, but I do have to work awfully hard, much harder than I would have to for Sutton, and he was so very nice to me. There is no money advantage either way.

Just as we were about to move back to our old billet, the boiler blew up again so I am still at the new hotel with most of everything in the way of clothes, etc. at the other place. It is a terrific nuisance and makes me feel rather as though I were in travel status.

Must go now and get a cup of coffee, then back to write a letter to Dad and Hannah, and by that time it will be noon and I will go to lunch and knock off for the rest of the day.

February 2, 1947[16]
Osaka, Japan

Dear Miss Warkentin,

We received your letter yesterday and were so delighted to hear from you and to hear that you are keeping fine in spite of your having been very busy at your office. I understand the heating was broken at your hotel and thereby you had to move temporarily somewhere. It must have been awful that the heating system got out of order in the height of severest cold season, especially in Tokyo, which is known for severe cold wind.

We were surprised to learn that Mimi has not yet seen you since his return to Tokyo at the middle of Jan., for he said before leaving our home that he would call you at an early opportunity. He must have been busy at school. I am writing him today to go to your office and see you at once. We are glad to hear that you will come to Kyoto again in March and looking forward to meeting you again. I advise you to come late in March and not before, because Kyoto is pretty cold until after the middle of March. It would be much better, if you can manage to put off your trip to around April 10th which is the best season in Kyoto. Of course, we are anxious to see you as soon as possible, but more anxious to let you see cherry blossoms in Kyoto.

The cherry season in Kyoto has no rival anywhere. Please let Mimi know as soon as you get travel orders. I understand you are going to Akakura for a week and am sure you will enjoy the trip. Chiyo asked me to convey her sincere regards.

Very sincerely yours, S. Kimura

---

16 S. Kimura letter, February 2, 1947.

17

Erna Decides to Leave the War Trials

February 27, 1947[17]

Dear "RJP",

This is not an easy letter to write. To give up this comfortable life of having the army take care of all your worries (well, almost all) to the cost of ten dollars a month for a nice room and 25 cents a meal and come back to slave again. Johnny was right!! However, they say one can stay in the Orient too long and eventually realities must be faced. So I've decided to come back and face you.

As you know, the trials are not yet over, defense having only begun its case. That means I have no choice but to finish my year, which will be the middle of May. I would like to make stops en route if that is possible. Civilians Personnel has not yet determined whether we will be allowed to do so. What I would like to do is cross over to Hong Kong and come down around Siam and India etc. How about asking your shipping friends if such a thing is possible? Some of the folks have heard that it is, but the tariff is pretty steep considering the length of time you can stay in each port. At any rate, I suspect I could arrange to be around by the time Mr. Higgenbotham leaves.

I have not forgotten the mission you gave me, but as yet have no good news for you. I am told that the only hope for Japan's economic recovery lies in what she can manufacture <u>here</u>, and that to send out any raw material would be detrimental even though, as you say, the manufactured article would be more successful if the work was done in the States. Pete McDermott heads up the Foreign Trade part of SCAP, and I read in the paper the other day that he is in New York City. Perhaps you could get

---

17 Erna Warkentin letter, February 27, 1947.

in touch with him there. I will try again to see if their policy has changed since I asked them last time I talked about it.

I'm afraid I haven't written as soon as you asked me to for your letters arrived in the midst of some junketing again. I took a weekend trip to Atami, a seaside resort called the "Riviera of Japan". It was truly lovely there and I would have liked to stay even longer, but the whole area is "off limits" and my invitation was only for Saturday and Sunday at the one Army Rest Hotel in the area. There was plum blossoms blooming and the air was mild. We saw oranges growing.

The past week I have been on annual leave up in the Japanese Alps, close to the Japan Sea at a place called Akakura. I even learned to ski, but I fear I will snow-plow the rest of my life.

At any rate, I came back without any sprains or broken bones. The latest report is that we had two broken ankles and several sprained ones in the group of some twenty-five who were learning the same week I was. The snow was ten feet deep and the scenery was perfectly lovely with mountains in every direction. We walked part way to the village one afternoon and came back on the ski-tow. We saw Japanese children who looked not more than three or four years old, on skis.

I have one more direction to cover, the island of Honshu. That is a long train trip and I'm not certain I'll get another leave period before May. Otherwise, I feel I've done pretty well about seeing this country. I know I

Akakura, February 18–24, 1947.

Erna in Akakura, February
18–24, 1947.

was supposed to get to China, but the War Department has always called that another "theater" and will not allow you to transfer from one theater to another. For a while they were allowing you to go over there for leave if you could give your guarantee about a place to stay and sufficient funds for food. Since our people are being pulled out almost entirely, even that is out. Of course I am somewhat concerned about a place to live when I get back to New York. If you or Miss Koezly hear of any place similar to what I had in Washington, keep me in mind. I have so many letters to write, I scarcely know how or when to do it.

We sent the boss home this afternoon because he had a very bad cold, and we are madly getting some of our personal correspondence done.

R.J. Paisley on right, Erna's boss in Washington DC and New York.

18

The Court Takes a Recess

March 3, 1947[18]

Dear Dorothy,

I suspect that I won't get very far on this, but I have tried and tried to get a letter off to you. I am back now from my week of annual leave, but we have been so busy we hardly know the time of day, and my portable typewriter at home is on the blink.

When I told you about working for Tavenner and his being a little higher up on the ladder than Sutton, I wasn't quite anticipating that he would be in effect the Acting Chief Prosecutor, but that is what he is for the time being so you can see that my office is Grand Central Station and in between keeping all the new attorneys informed, the old ones in line and the tremendous number of papers in order that keep pouring in, I really do have to cheat to write a letter.

I wrote one letter the other day, had been putting it off for three weeks. Paisley wrote me some time ago. I got the letter the weekend I went to Atami. He asked first for me to cable and then said it would be all right to airmail my reply as to whether I still wanted to work for him and if so, when I would be returning. Thought it was darn nice of him to keep the job open indefinitely as he has.

I am ready to come home and have decided the tempo of New York City is probably the most apt to keep me contented in the U.S.A., and then too, his job is still closely allied with foreign interests. So, I told him that I thought I could be around about June 30. It is going to be a bit difficult to give up the easy living here, the nice fat bank account I am building up, the inexpensive rate of living <u>and</u> the front row seat at the trials; but I

---

18 Erna Warkentin letter, March 3, 1947.

Presentation to the Tribunal of new members of the IPS, March 3, 1947.

Presentation to the Tribunal of new members
of the IPS - 4 March 1947...

Reading from left to right:

1. Hsueh-yi Wu, China
2. Dant Ho China
3. Judson seyi, china
4. Lloyd W. Cunningham USA.
5. Robert Williley U.S.A.
6. Smith N. Crowe Jr.-U.
7. Foster Dunngan USA
8. Cay Rueland High W
9. Thomas F. Mornane, Australia

Presentation to the Tribunal of new members of the IPS,
March 3, 1947.

gathered from Paiseley's letter that he wanted now to make the permanent plans about the reorganization of his office and that in all fairness I couldn't expect him to wait for me forever.

I think I wrote you last just before I went to Atami. The weekend turned out to be a very nice one. The hotel itself is lovely and nestled among hills on the bay. The weather is much warmer there due to the current in the bay and there were plum blossoms and oranges all over the place. Saturday afternoon we took a long drive around the Izu Peninsula and saw a lot of beautiful scenery and interesting sights. We came back and took a hot mineral bath and then joined the boys to drink beer and do a little dancing. Another girl I know and I hit upon two very nice lads who insisted upon taking us walking and shopping the next morning. We were out

Erna on train to ski Akakura.

all morning and took lots of pictures. After lunch we took another mineral bath and lazed around for a while and caught the mid-afternoon train back.

My annual leave plans fitted in beautifully with the recess of the court. Mr. Tavenner said I couldn't have picked a better week to be gone. I took off from Tokyo at 8 o'clock in the morning and the trip took until well past 4 in the afternoon. We were met at the train in Teguchi by weazels, a funny kind of vehicle which can travel in water or over deep snow, sort of like a caterpillar. We drove for about half an hour up a mountain to the hotel, which is set up on top of the mountain, Lord of all it surveys. We were starved for we had only provided ourselves with candy and a couple pieces of fruit, thinking there would be a diner on the train. It seemed like heaven to have a nice drink and sit down to a steak dinner which was out of this world. The first time I've had a steak put before just the way I like it without having ordered it so.

Couldn't get ski shoes the next morning, so I ploughed around some on snow shoes and took one of those hot baths again. There was nine feet of snow and it snowed all afternoon and night and for the most part of the following two days. The next morning I had ski shoes and managed the snow-plough perfectly but could never seem to get my courage up enough to master the various turns. I fear I will snow-plough the rest of my life, but I don't mind too much since those who became more proficient at the art came home with all sorts of injuries. There were two broken ankles and several bad sprains; someone said the average was one injury per day.

Seems to me there is too much risk involved and too much hard work climbing the hill, for the brief thrill of sliding down again. At any rate I did have a lot of fun and I do now know what it is all about. Stayed up there a week and had lots of good food, played quite a bit of bridge, had suki-yaki dinners and the Japanese hot baths. I hated having to come back to work.

The package I sent you included a dark kimono from the Kimura's, the pj's Sutton brought back from China and the summer kimono was given to me by some Japanese people I met in Karuizawa this summer.

I was amused at the Efficiency Rating given to me. It was the first time I have had anything but excellent. I guess its best I get out of the government. If I find a nice place to live in New York, I think that should be pretty much ok as I could see you quite a bit and you could come to see me, too. I told Paiseley to tell his staff to keep their eyes and ears open, you, too.

Erna on ski trip to Akakura.

(Above and below) Erna on ski trip to Akakura.

March 11, 1947[19]

Dear Dorothy,

You should see our new money. It is mostly a brilliant fuschia shade. They suddenly called in our military script at ten o'clock yesterday morning and gave us this new stuff today. Seems the black market is really operating in that line. Someone in our office had a Japanese approach him the other day offering to sell him military script for yen. The fellow acquired the yen through sale of cigarettes, etc. This American asked the Japanese how many dollars he had and he told him $1000. No Japanese has any reason whatsoever for possessing <u>any</u> military script.

They say it is even worse in Germany where they are even counterfeiting the stuff and the main reason our money here was changed was to shut down that black market and avoid the old military script being sent here as a way out. You see all occupied areas use the same stuff, no indication as to which country it was issued in. It was amazing to everyone who the powers that be kept it such a secret. Only the absolutely necessary people knew of the change until ten yesterday and the new money was ready to be distributed. Surely must have caught the Japanese and Germans short. I must get back to work again.

---

19 Erna Warkentin letter, March 11, 1947.

19

Erna Sees Hiroshima Destruction

March 21, 1947[20]

Father William Kleinsorge
Catholic Church
Hiroshima, Japan

Dear Father Kleinsorge:
Miss Erna Warkentin, Miss Mary Friedman, and Miss Olga Stefanelli are three very good friends of mine. All three are employed by the International Prosecution Section. I told them about my recent trip to Hiroshima and the very interesting visit I had with you and the other good Fathers. I am sure they will have the same appreciation I had if you can extend to them similar courtesies to those you extended to me.

Lt. Fleischer and myself will feel very disappointed if you ever come to Tokyo and do not pay us a visit.

Sincerely yours,
Edward P. Monaghan
Assistant Chief
Investigation Division

---

20 Edward P. Monaghan letter, March 21, 1947.

April 10, 1947[21]

Dear Dorothy,

It doesn't seem possible that I haven't written you for so long, and I don't have the carbon of my last letter here, but I feel pretty sure I haven't told you about my trip to Hiroshima two weekends ago, my trip to Kyoto the next one and my trip to Karuizawa this past weekend. That in itself will indicate to you that I haven't been standing still for very much of the time.

Three of us girls took the night train down to Kura where the British are stationed. Telephone arrangements supposedly made for our stay in advance. We arrived there to find things a bit mixed up, and an Australian captain took over. He failed to arrange overnight accommodations so we thought best to come back again on the night train and made reservations accordingly. We arrived about three in the afternoon. He took his driver and we drove over to Hiroshima and saw quite a bit of the place. At least all I wanted to for I was only interested in seeing myself just what one bomb could do.

It was amazing. They have done considerable rebuilding in the way of one story wooden buildings, but there is still devastation over a vast area and it seems incredible that one bomb did it all.

It was incredible and very frightening indeed. I

Erna's visit to Hiroshima, March 1947.

had a letter of introduction to Father Klinesorge (New Yorker magazine article and survivor of the Atom bomb dropped on Hiroshima). Our time was limited for we had driven about the town quite some time to locate the monastery so when we found he was down at the church in town we had to give up talking to him personally.

---

21 Erna Warkentin letter, April 10, 1947.

We did, however, talk with a Father Schiffer who was also mentioned in that (and also survived the Atom bomb). He was the priest with all the shattered glass in his back that they carried to the monastery on one of the two available litters. He speaks English very well and told us quite a bit about the actual happenings, none of which were new to us since we had read the article, but it was most interesting indeed to meet someone like that. We drove back to Kure just in time for dinner and spent the evening drinking Black & White scotch. At dinner word came that there were only two reservations on the night train, to sum it up, I took that train and the other two girls waited until the next day.

Erna's visit to Hiroshima, March 1947.

It was especially important that I be back to work on time and I couldn't afford to take the chances on reservations the next day. The evening in Hiroshima was a lot of fun.

Australian, English, Welsh and New Zealand officers, and I expect the girls down there could boil us in oil for none of them would leave the bar and go to the officers club since we didn't want to go ourselves. The captain who took us to Hiroshima had just come back from a ten day official trip and he ignored reporting in, etc. just to squire us around. They were the nicest, friendliest people I have ever met and invited us down for another weekend, promising to get all our clearances for us, reservations, etc.

They planned for the weekend they have their big dance and said they would take us for a launch trip around the Inland Sea and over to Hiroshima again. We arranged for six girls to go down and I put the call through this morning to find that the Capt. whom I was supposed to call was not in and the one who answered the phone remembering me perfectly and reminding me that he was one of the two who drove me to the station. I was sorry indeed to inform him I couldn't come this time. The other one (who with this one have complete charge of all the facilities required for such trips) had asked me to be his personal guest.

However, it is an 18 hour train trip each way and the cherry blossoms are out around here, so....also it would mean a day away from work and I don't want to ask for that now since I want to take one more long trip before I leave.

This is five days later and it is the first chance I have had to get back to this letter. I will do my utmost to finish it this afternoon.

The next weekend I again had orders to go to Kyoto. I didn't look forward to the trip because I knew I then had to cope once and for all the delivery of the package to the Kimura's, a problem which had been causing me no end of worry since the restrictions as to giving gifts requested from the States specifically had become a very dangerous thing. This is due of course to the practice of many people ordering for the specific purpose of selling at exorbitant sums of on the black market. It is quite all right for a Japanese to request something himself, for then the censors and customs have some control and it all very definitely comes under the heading of charity. I asked any number of people who understood my position and they all considered the package "hot".

Mr. Sutton fully expected that before it was all done someone would have to get up in court one day and explain that Mr. Tavenner was absent because he was trying to get me out of the 8th Army Stockade.

I probably have enough influential friends to explain my motives, but my main worry was the cloud of suspicion hanging over the Kimura's when the whole family blossomed out in new, undeniably state-side shoes all of a sudden, especially since Mimi is most anxious to get a job in the capacity of a translator with the allied powers.

I finally got ahold of the Chaplain, thinking he might give me a lead of charity avenue, thus having some sort of endorsement. He knew none, but suggested that I go ahead, being careful not to take a big parcel which would attract attention. I packed up the girl's shoes and a couple of my old dresses in my traveling bag, taking only a minimum amount of clothes for myself. Mimi and his father called for me at the hotel and we rode on the train to their home, which is half way between Osaka and Kobe. Mr. Kimura thought I might again be able to get them on the military coach, but I didn't dare take the chance. As a matter of fact an MP carried my bag to the train.

Their coach was so crowded they barely got on, but they had given me a chart so I had no trouble getting off at the same station they did. We walked to their home from there and along the sea wall; they live in a lovely section, facing the water with mountains at their back.

I understand the climate is probably the most desirable in Honshu. We had a nice suki-yaki dinner and talked for a while. Mr. Kimura was insistent that I bring back with me, as a gift, a lovely Takimono by a famous Japanese artist, but I declined that principally because I could not afford to have anyone think I had been "bartering", which is also illegal; also because I am becoming more and more embarrassed at explaining why I can't do more for them than I can.

Truly, I am not being a sissy about this. I know a charming Nisei girl who scarcely sees her relatives over here because they want her to do things she can't. Mr. Kimura wanted to take me around Osaka so we left around 3:30 and went to his office where we picked up the office electric car and drove around for an hour. Osaka was heavily bombed and Mr. Kimura is having to use part of his office as a warehouse. Mimi and I went back to Kyoto around six.

A card given to Erna by Hiroshima atomic bomb survivor
Father Hubert Schiffer on church card.

Erna and the Kimura family.

My suspicions were first aroused when I checked the track number in the RTO and found an MP stationed at a desk above which was a sign to the effect that he was there to check travel orders. We went through a Japanese gate and up to the train and no one stopped us. However, when I got back here I was telling about my trip, and our Executive Officer's secretary asked how in the world I had gotten to Osaka since no one from GHQ was supposed to go unless they were on official business! She has wanted to go ever since she has been here. My absolute innocence and air of having twelve copies of orders in my purse must have bluffed everybody, thank God.

I have yet to deliver the boys shoes, and I guess I'm stuck with it for the Browns and Everts both wrote to the Kimura's asking if they had received the various items!!! The censors removed a newspaper clipping from Mr. Brown's last letter to Mr. Kimura, so they are still on the job. There are friends of mine here in Tokyo who won't let me leave town unless they are along, and needless to say, I am not giving travel talks on Osaka.

Easter weekend we had an extra day off, Army Day on Monday. Since all the rest hotels near Tokyo are filled with dependents awaiting housing it is becoming almost impossible to go away weekends for Japanese homes and hotels are all off limits now, for overnight stays. Mr. Tavenner called a friend of his who "arranged" for four of us to stay at one of the rest hotels in Karuizawa so we took the train early Saturday morning and came back on the four o'clock train Monday afternoon. The only Protestant services were in a Japanese church, and again the "amens" and the songs gave me an idea of the progress of the service, plus the help of an English speaking Japanese.

It is rather a impressive sight to attend a service like that. The same service you have always known, the devout faces of all the Japanese, especially when you know the history of the Christian religion in Japan and know that there were periods when they suffered tortures and martyrdom equal to the early Christians in Rome, and as lately as during this last war they must have had to take cover. Most of the weekend was spent in a leisurely way, walks in the beautiful sunshine, a mineral bath in a Japanese bath house, lots of excellent food (at 25 cent a meal) and good company.

The past ten days the cherry blossoms have been beautiful and thanks to Mr. Tavenner, who has given me two rolls of colored film I have been recording some of it. Saturday afternoon we went out to Ueno Park and Sunday we went to Kamikura. This coming weekend we are plotting a trip for all day Sunday from Tokyo to Myanoshita across the mountains to Yamanaka, having Sunday dinner (at noon) at either the Fujiyea or FujiView Hotel. The blossoms are supposed to be out in the valleys on that trip across the mountain range, and truly a sight to behold. Keep your fingers crossed, we are not yet certain of transportation.

I have been weighing seriously the advisability of delaying my departure until the middle of June. I haven't had a response from Mr. Paisley yet and my idea is to plan for that unless I hear from him that he would definitely dislike

The Kimura family.

the idea. My reasoning is that it is nice here in June so why waste it all on a boat trip which would be just as comfortable a month later that I originally planned. Of course Tavenner hit the ceiling when I told him the time was approaching. He concentrates on his work to the extent that he had just assumed I would be here forever and ever. I can't say that working for him is hard to take either. He has been very nice to me and I admire him very much. I seem to hit some pretty swell people to work for. He teases me about my boyfriend, and if they ever meet I'm sure I'll have a time sticking to my plans to leave in June.

Best I get in my "requests" and sign off. Luck has been with me so far, but it can't last forever and Tavenner is apt to come up from the courtroom at any time.

20

Erna Prepares To Leave Japan

In General Macarthur's farewell address to the US Congress in April 1951, MacArthur commented on his trust in the Japanese and stated that Japan had undergone one of the greatest reformations in modern history, claiming that its people had left the ashes of World War II and erected an "edifice" built in tribute to the "supremacy of individual liberty and personal dignity." MacArthur said, "I know of no nation more serene, orderly, and industrious, nor in which higher hopes can be entertained for future constructive service in the advance of the human race."

Acting Chief Prosecutor Frank Tavenner Jr., Mitsui House, January 1947.

April 30, 1947[22]

Dear Dorothy,

Time seems to be getting dreadfully short for all that I still would like to do, outside the office. Tavenner has finally become convinced I won't be persuaded to stay longer, and bless his heart, he feels pretty bad about it. Don't think I could stand the pace at the office much longer though, I have to have an extra girl practically all the time and the both of us are constantly going around in circles.

---

22 Erna Warkentin letter, April 30, 1947.

I am going to my last Nippon Philharmonic Concert tonight. They only play one evening concert a month and I just can't see being indoors on Sunday afternoons now that the weather is nice again.

I have tentative plans which I really shouldn't even mention yet for taking a trip to Shanghai, Manila and Hong Kong. It is a trip which requires twenty some days, with stops at those three places of from two to four days each. I am on the list for the May 31 sailing, but they can't tell until the boat leaves San Francisco the middle of May whether they will have space enough. It is only a slim chance, but I thought worthwhile waiting for.

Will be sending off a box within the next few days of a lot of stuff I had to give my room "atmosphere", plus some beautiful material given to me. Just leave the box intact. There will be another shortly of all my winter clothes, and then I think one more will complete the job. I expect you are wondering what I am going to do with all my stuff when I get home. Well I am too. Best I stop now. The work isn't anywhere near finished. It just never is any more.

Erna in Japan, 1947.

May 1947

I wish to express my gratitude for you were so kind for me during you stayed in Japan. I am very sad to miss you from Japan. But I hope, you will come back again to Japan someday. Goodbye. Good luck!

Your maid

On June 2, 1947, Erna departed Yokohama, Japan on the U.S.S. General Shanks. She arrived in Seattle on June 21, 1947. This young lady from Beatrice, Nebraska had managed to put herself in the middle of some of the most historical events in American history.

Erna returns home on *USS Shanks* June 2, 1947.

Erna returns home on
USS Shanks June 2, 1947.

Erna returns home
on *USS Shanks* June
21, 1947.

21

Erna Arrives Home

July 24, 1947[23]

Dear Mr. Tavenner,

I am finally re-establishing in the importing brokerage business in New York City, and am finding the work very interesting. I have by no means forgotten Tokyo and the trials, and I have often wondered just how you are getting along. This is very different indeed from a law office.

I had a nice, long letter from Miss Wiehle yesterday in which she mentioned that Mrs. Tavenner had arrived and that you had taken a week off. I am very glad she has come for I was certain she would be able to get you away from the terrific grind for periods of much needed rest.

Other letters from Japan have told me of the six-week recess and how you spent it. Even though it was quite a job I know the disposal of those prisoners was always a problem you were anxious to straighten out.

I had a very nice trip home and spent two weeks in Washington before coming to New York. During those two weeks I had a chance to visit some of our old friends. Took the opportunity to scold Mr. Hyde for not being in Tokyo to help you, and, of course, received the assurance that he would be only too glad to be with you if the necessary arrangements could be made. He is keeping quite busy and seemed his usual cheerful self. I also had lunch one day with Miss Kato, Miss Anderson and Mrs. McKinney, all of whom asked about you. They were looking fine, and it was good to exchange news bits with all of them.

I suppose you have forgotten about the pictures I promised to send you. However, I did not forget and here they are. The one of Miss Wiehle and

23 Erna Warkentin letter, July 24, 1947.

the cherry blossoms is on the drive into the War Ministry grounds, and the other cherry blossom pictures are from Ueno Park.

I want to tell you again how much I enjoyed working with you in Tokyo. Perhaps when you and Mrs. Tavenner return to the States you will come to New York. If so, I should love to see you and hear all about the trials in Tokyo as of the date I left Japan.

Sincerely yours,
Erna Warkentin

P.S. Please give my regards to the Mitsui House folks, and tell Mr. Wiley I was very sorry not to have the chance to say goodbye to him. Please also say "hello" to Mr. Sutton,

EW

Erna would eventually marry Tom Shelton, a medical officer in the U.S. Army and they returned to Japan in the 1950's while Tom was stationed there. They eventually transferred to Germany where they adopted their only daughter, Betsy. Erna and Tom spent their final years living in Merced, CA. Upon Erna's death in 2000, she would be buried beside her husband in Arlington National Cemetery. Erna would never forget her experiences with the JIOA in Germany and the Tokyo War Trials in Japan. In later years she never discussed it. In 2017 a treasure trove of historical documents, letters, photographs and artifacts were discovered in her three trunks including the trunk she used in 1945 – 1947. Everything was in perfect condition. In addition to the above, Erna preserved a huge collection of Tokyo Trial passes and documents, Japanese woodblock prints, kimonos, pottery, etc. As a young lady from the beautiful town of Beatrice, Nebraska, Erna Elizabeth Warkentin dreamed of a better and more rewarding life. Her time spent in Germany and Japan would thrust her into some of the most historical events in American and world history. And although the voices of the past are long gone, we can still dream of the days that were and we can remember this amazing generation that saved the world and helped to keep America safe for future generations.

Erna sunbathing in Tokyo.